BETTY ROOT

Mein erstes englisches Wörterbuch

My First English Dictionary

Illustriert von
Jonathan Langley

Weltbild

A B C D E F G H I J K L M N O P Q R S T U V W X Y Z

Dorling DK Kindersley

Inhalt

Vorwort für Eltern, Lehrerinnen und Lehrer   3

Die englische Originalausgabe
erschien 1993 unter dem Titel
My First Dictionary
bei Dorling Kindersley Limited, London

Genehmigte Lizenzausgabe der
Verlagsgruppe Weltbild GmbH,
Steinerne Furt, D-86167 Augsburg
Copyright der englischen Originalausgabe
© 1993 by Dorling Kindersley Limited, London
Copyright der deutschsprachigen Ausgabe
© 2001 by Dorling Kindersley Verlag GmbH,
München
Übersetzung: Klaus Karwat
Fachliche Beratung und Vorwort:
Gisela Schultz-Steinbach,
Aus- und Fortbilderin für Englisch an der
Grund- und Hauptschule am
IPTS Regionalseminar Neumünster
Umschlaggestaltung:
coverdesign uhlig, bobingen
Umschlagmotive: Dorling Kindersley
Gesamtherstellung: Neografia, a.s.,
Škultètyho 1, SK-03655 Martin
Printed in Slovakia
ISBN 3-8289-2052-7

2007   2006   2005
Die letzte Jahreszahl gibt
die aktuelle Lizenzausgabe an.

Besuchen Sie uns im Internet:
www.weltbild.de

The English dictionary –
Englisches Wörterbuch   4

Dictionary games –
Wörterbuch-Spiele   92

Englisch-deutsches Wortregister   96

Vorwort für Eltern, Lehrerinnen und Lehrer

My First English Dictionary ist vielleicht das erste englische Wörterbuch, das Ihr Kind bzw. Ihre Schülerinnen und Schüler in den Händen halten. Durch **eindeutig gestaltete Illustrationen und ausgewählte** Fotos können sich schon die Jüngsten die Bedeutung der über 1000 aufgelisteten englischen Wörter erschließen. Der hier angebotene **Wortschatz aus der alltäglichen Lebenswirklichkeit und kindlichen Erfahrungswelt entspricht den Erkenntnissen und Forderungen des modernen einsprachigen Fremdsprachenunterrichts in der Grundschule** und wurde mit Lernanfängern erprobt.

Zu Beginn des Lernprozesses, der auf kommunikative Bewältigung von Alltagssituationen abzielt, steht zunächst die Ausbildung der Kompetenz des Hörverstehens und der damit verbundene **passive Wortschatz** an erster Stelle. Für seinen erfolgreichen Aufbau und seine Festigung müssen den unterschiedlichen Lerntypen unter den Kindern möglichst vielfältige Impulse geboten werden. Dazu eignen sich besonders gut **Lernangebote mit farbigen Bildern**. In der Praxis hat sich herausgestellt, dass viele Kinder nicht nur auf optische Reize in Form von Bildern, sondern auch auf Wortbilder positiv reagieren. Die Verbindung aus **erklärendem Bild und englischem Wort** in diesem Wörterbuch kann deshalb den Lernprozess positiv unterstützen.

Zunächst werden Kinder beginnen, in dem Buch zu blättern und zu forschen. Bei diesen eher zufälligen Streifzügen durch das Wörterbuch entwickelt sich ganz behutsam die **Grundlage für ein Sprachgefühl**. Kinder erkennen die Ähnlichkeiten mit der Muttersprache und finden Anglizismen, die sie aus ihrer eigenen Lernumgebung kennen. Sie entdecken den Unterschied, wie ein Wort lautet und wie es geschrieben wird. Damit wird die **Basis für eine solide Sprachbeherrschung** gelegt, die bei allen Lernenden individuell sehr unterschiedlich verläuft.

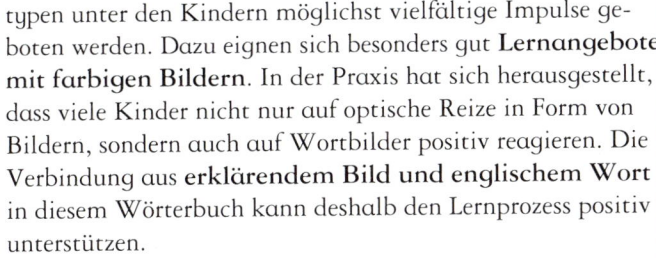

Danach werden Kinder gezielt die im Unterricht erlernten und geübten Lautbilder den Schriftbildern zuordnen wollen. Sie sammeln immer mehr Erfahrungen im Einsatz von englischen Wörtern in Alltagssituationen, die nachgespielt und -gesprochen werden. So bauen sie sich ihren Individualsprachschatz auf, der die Voraussetzung für eine sichere mündliche wie schriftliche Sprachproduktion darstellt. Wann Kinder beginnen, sich im **aktiven Sprachgebrauch** zu üben, ist individuell sehr unterschiedlich und sollte keinesfalls erzwungen werden.

In Anlehnung an das Prinzip des einsprachigen Englischunterrichts, der Kinder auf möglichst natürliche Weise auf die authentische Kommunikationssituation mit einer englischsprachigen Person vorbereiten will, bietet dieses Wörterbuch auch für die nächste Stufe des Fremdsprachenlernprozesses, auf der mehr und mehr das Lesen und Schreiben hinzu kommen, **kurze englische Erklärungstexte** an. Diese sollen zunächst vorgelesen werden, um das Verstehen der Lernenden zu schulen. Danach stellen sie für

die Kinder Quellen dar, mit deren Hilfe sie sich um ein erstes Erfassen bemühen können. Die Kinder werden je nach Lerntyp und persönlicher Neigung selbst entscheiden, ob bzw. in welchem Maße sie sich mit der Entschlüsselung der Texte befassen wollen.

Im Anhang können alle illustrierten englischen Wörter sowie Wörter aus den Erklärungstexten in einem alphabetischen **Register** nachgeschlagen werden, wo neben der **deutschen Übersetzung** auch – als Vorlesehilfe für Eltern oder ältere Kinder – die **Lautschrift** zu finden ist. **Ideen zu kreativen Übungsspielen** mit den Buchelementen helfen, den aktiven und passiven Wortschatz der Kinder zu sichern und sie mit dem Gebrauch eines Wörterbuches vertraut zu machen.

A B C D E F G H I J K L M N O P Q R S T U V W X Y Z

A

Aa *Aa* Aa Aa

above

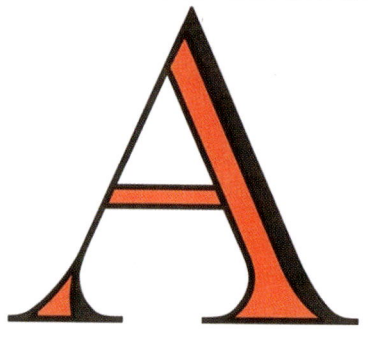

When something is **above** something else, it is higher up. These birds are flying above the trees.

accident

An **accident** is something that happens by mistake.

acrobat

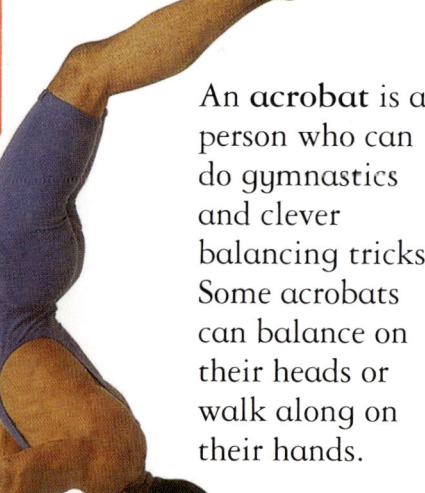

An **acrobat** is a person who can do gymnastics and clever balancing tricks. Some acrobats can balance on their heads or walk along on their hands.

act

To **act** is to pretend to be someone else. An **actor** is a person who acts in a play in front of an audience. Some actors act in television programmes and films.

add

To **add** is to find the sum total of two or more numbers.

address

An **address** is the number of the building, and the name of the street and the town where a person lives or works.

adult

An **adult** is a grown-up person. Men and women are adults. When you are older, you will become an adult.

aeroplane

An **aeroplane** is a flying machine with wings. It flies people and packages quickly from one place to another.

airport

An **airport** is a place where aeroplanes take off and land.

alligator

An **alligator** is a reptile with thick, scaly skin and lots of sharp teeth.

alphabet

abcdefg
English alphabet

абвгдеж
Russian alphabet

An **alphabet** is a list of all the letters we use to write words. Different languages have different alphabets.

a b c d e f g h i j k l m n o p q r s t u v w x y z

ambulance

An **ambulance** is a special vehicle that is used to carry sick or injured people to a hospital.

anchor

An **anchor** is a large, metal hook on a long chain. It digs into the bottom of the sea to stop a ship moving.

angry

An **angry** person is someone who feels very cross about something.

animal

An **animal** is any living thing that is not a plant. You are an animal, and so is a fish, a spider, a bird, a snake, and a dog.

fish, spider, bird, snake, dog, girl

ant

An **ant** is a tiny insect. Ants live in nests under the ground.

ape

An **ape** is a large monkey without a tail.

apple

An **apple** is a fruit that grows on an apple tree.

aquarium

An **aquarium** is a tank of water for keeping fish in. You can watch the fish as they swim around.

arm

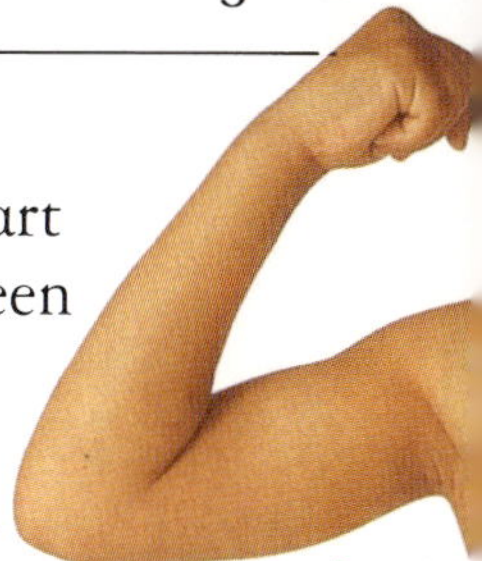

Your **arm** is the part of your body between your shoulder and your hand.

armadillo

An **armadillo** is an animal covered with hard, bony scales. These scales protect the armadillo from attack.

armour

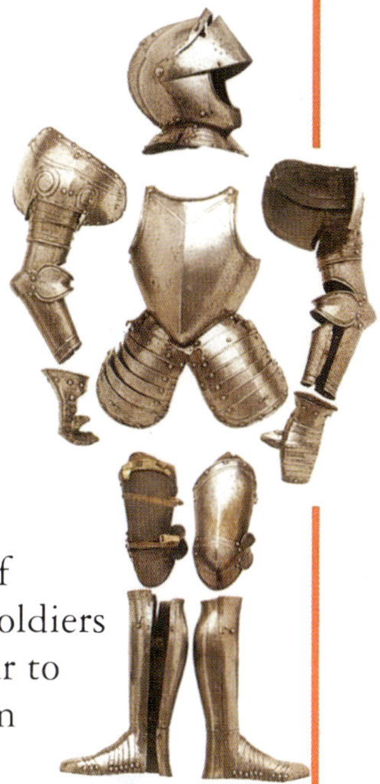

Armour is a suit made of metal. Hundreds of years ago, soldiers wore armour to protect them in battle.

army

An **army** is a large group of soldiers who are trained to fight on land in times of war.

5

A B C D E F G H I J K L M N O P Q R S T U V W X Y Z

arrow
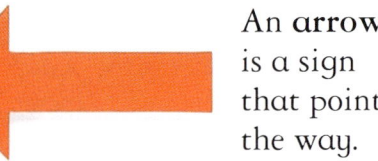
An **arrow** is a sign that points the way.

artist

An **artist** is a person who makes beautiful things. Some artists draw or paint pictures. Other artists make pots out of clay, or statues out of stone.

astronaut

An **astronaut** is a person who travels in outer space. Some astronauts have walked on the moon or launched space satellites.

athlete

An **athlete** is a person who is good at sports such as running, jumping, and swimming. Athletes take part in races or competitions.

audience

An **audience** is a group of people watching a play or listening to a concert.

author

An **author** is a person who writes stories, poems, or plays.

avalanche
An **avalanche** is a sudden fall of snow and rocks down the side of a mountain.

B
Bb *Bb* Bb *Bb*

baby

A **baby** is a very young child.

back

The **back** of something is the part behind the front.

back
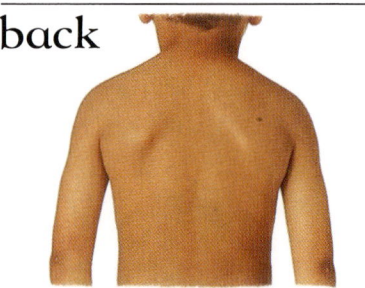
Your **back** is the part of your body that is behind your chest. Your back is between your neck and your bottom.

bake

To **bake** something is to cook it in an oven. A **baker** is a person who makes bread and cakes in a **bakery**.

a **b** c d e f g h i j k l m n o p q r s t u v w x y z

ball
A **ball** is used to play some games and sports. Most balls are round.

balloon
A **balloon** is a thin rubber bag that is blown up with air or another kind of gas.

banana
A **banana** is a long, curved fruit with a yellow skin. Bananas grow in bunches on banana plants.

band
A **band** is a group of people playing musical instruments together.

bandage
A **bandage** is a strip of material that is used to cover an injury.

bank

A **bank** is the high ground on both sides of a river or a stream.

bank

A **bank** is a safe place where you can keep money. You can take your money out again when you need it.

barbecue

A **barbecue** is a meal you cook outside on an open fire.

barn

A **barn** is a large farm building where a farmer keeps machinery or animals.

baseball

Baseball is a game played with a bat and ball by two teams of nine players.

basket
A **basket** is a kind of container for carrying things.

bat
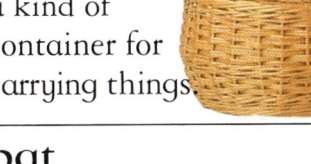
A **bat** is a kind of stick that you use to hit a ball.

A B C D E F G H I J K L M N O P Q R S T U V W X Y Z

bat

A **bat** is a small, furry animal with wings. Bats hang upside down to sleep during the day. They hunt for food at night.

bath
A **bath** is a tub that you fill with water and sit in to wash yourself. A **bathroom** is the room where you take a bath.

battery

A **battery** is a sealed case that makes electricity for torches and toys.

beach

A **beach** is the strip of land by the edge of the sea. Beaches are covered with sand or pebbles.

beak

A **beak** is the hard, pointed part of a bird's mouth.

bear
A **bear** is a large, heavy animal with thick fur and strong claws.

beard
A **beard** is the hair that grows on a man's chin and cheeks.
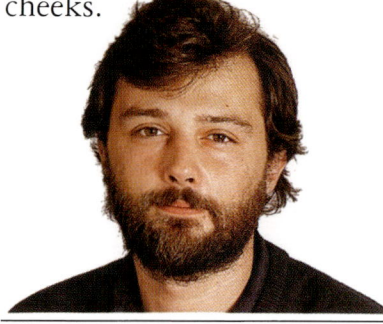

bed
A **bed** is a piece of furniture that you sleep on. A **bedroom** is the room where you go to sleep.

bee

A **bee** is a flying insect. Some bees collect nectar, the sweet liquid in flowers, and turn it into honey.

beetle
A **beetle** is a flying insect. Beetles have hard, shiny wing cases to protect the soft parts of their bodies.

behind

When something is **behind** something else, it is at the back of it. This boy is hiding behind the curtains.

bell
A **bell** is a hollow piece of metal shaped like a cup. When you shake a bell, it rings.

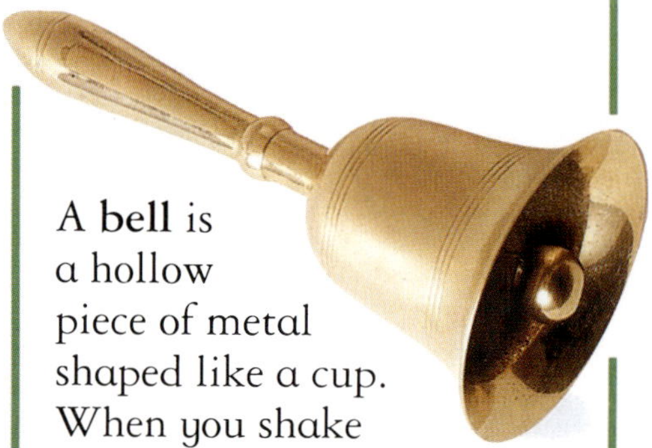

a b c d e f g h i j k l m n o p q r s t u v w x y z

below
When something is **below** something else, it is lower down. This bulb is growing below the surface of the soil.

belt

A **belt** is a strap that you wear around your waist.

bench
A **bench** is a seat for more than one person.

berry

A **berry** is a soft, juicy, stoneless fruit.

between

When you are **between** two things, you are standing in the middle of them.

bicycle
A **bicycle** is a machine with two wheels that are moved round by pedals. To ride a **bike** you sit on the seat, pedal with your feet, and steer using the handlebars.

handlebar
seat
pedal
wheel

big

When something is **big**, it is not small. This shirt is too big for this girl.

binoculars

Binoculars are a special kind of glasses. They make things that are far away look bigger and closer.

bird
A **bird** is an animal with feathers, two wings, and a beak. Most birds can fly.

birthday
Your **birthday** is the day of the year when you were born. You may get **birthday cards** and eat **birthday cake** on this special day.

bite
To **bite** something is to take hold of it with your teeth.

black
Black is a very dark colour. It is the opposite of white.

9

A **B** C D E F G H I J K L M N O P Q R S T U V W X Y Z

blanket

A **blanket** is a thick cloth that keeps you warm in bed.

blind
To be **blind** is to have difficulty seeing. **Guide dogs** help blind people to walk about safely.

blood
Blood is the red liquid that is pumped around your body by your heart.

blossom

Blossom is the flower that grows on a fruit tree.

blouse

A **blouse** is a garment worn by a girl or a woman on the top part of her body.

blow
To **blow** is to push air quickly out of your mouth. This girl is blowing bubbles.

blue

Blue is the colour of the sky on a sunny day.

boat
A **boat** is a small ship. Boats carry people and cargo across the water.

body
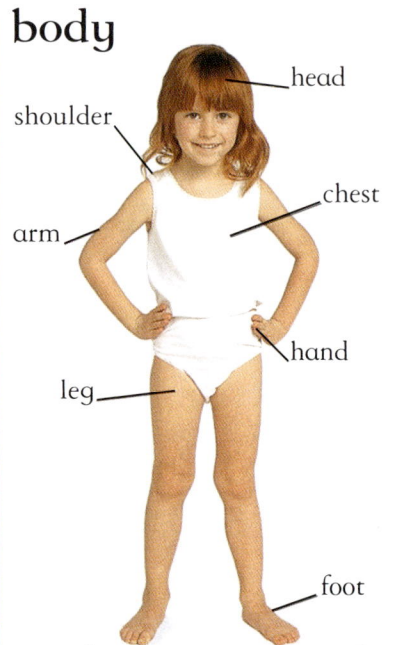
shoulder, head, arm, chest, hand, leg, foot

Your **body** is every part of you.

bone
A **bone** is one of the pieces of a skeleton. You have 206 different bones in your body.

book

A **book** is a collection of pages held together between two covers. There are words and pictures printed on the pages of a book.

boomerang

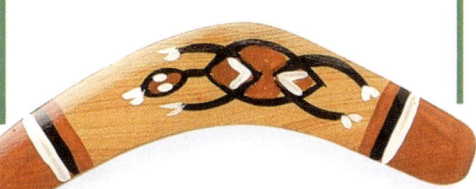

A **boomerang** is a flat, curved piece of wood. When you throw a boomerang, it turns around in the air and comes back to you.

bottle

A **bottle** is a glass or plastic container for drinks and other liquids.

bottom

The **bottom** of something is the lowest part of it.

bowl

A **bowl** is a deep, round dish to put food in.

box

A **box** is a container with straight sides, a bottom, and sometimes a top.

boy

A **boy** is a male child.

brain

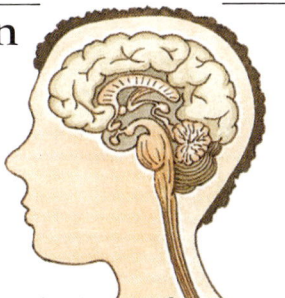

Your **brain** is inside your head. You think with your brain, and it controls your body.

branch

A **branch** is the part of a tree that grows from the tree trunk.

branch
tree trunk

bread

Bread is a food that is made from a mixture of water, flour or meal, and sometimes yeast.

break

When something **breaks**, it cracks into pieces.

breakfast

Breakfast is the first meal that you eat in the day.

brick

A **brick** is a block of baked, hard clay used for building.

bride

A **bride** is a woman who is getting married. The man she is marrying is the **bridegroom**. After the wedding, they are **wife** and **husband**.

bridge

A **bridge** is a road that is built over rivers or railways so that people can get across.

brown

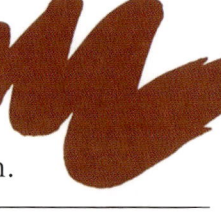

Brown is a colour. Wood and soil are brown.

brush

A **brush** is a tool that has a lot of bristles. A **hair-brush** is used to brush your hair. Other kinds of brushes are used to sweep or paint with.

bucket

A **bucket** is a container with a handle that is used to hold water or other things.

bud

A **bud** is a young leaf or flower before it opens.

building

A **building** is a place, with walls and a roof, where people live or work. **Builders** use bricks, concrete, stones, or wood to **build** buildings.

bulb

A **bulb** is the part of a plant that grows underground.

bulb

A **bulb** is the glass part of an electric lamp that gives out light.

bulldozer

A **bulldozer** is a powerful machine that is used to move heavy rocks and soil on a building site.

burglar

A **burglar** is a person who breaks into a building to steal something.

burn

To **burn** something is to set it on fire.

bus

A **bus** is a large vehicle that carries a lot of people. The **bus driver** stops at a **bus-stop** to let the passengers get on and off.

a b c d e f g h i j k l m n o p q r s t u v w x y z

butcher

A **butcher** is a person who cuts up meat and sells it.

butter

Butter is a yellow, fatty food that is made from cream.

butterfly

A **butterfly** is a flying insect with four colourful wings.

button

A **button** is a small, round object used for fastening clothes.

buy
To **buy** is to give money for something so that it belongs to you. The blond boy is buying a ball.

C

Cc Cc Cc Cc

cabbage
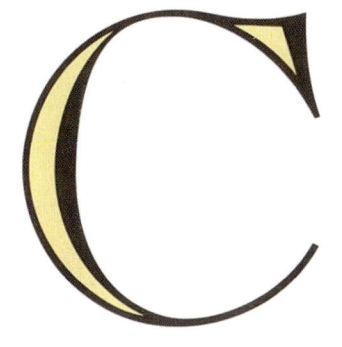
A **cabbage** is a vegetable with tightly packed leaves.

cabin

A **cabin** is a wooden house, often made from logs.

cactus
A **cactus** is a prickly plant that grows in the desert. A cactus stores water in its thick stem.

calculator

A **calculator** is a machine that you use to work with numbers.

calendar

A **calendar** is a chart that shows you what day it is. Calendars also show the month and the year.

camel

A **camel** is a large animal with one or two humps on its back. Camels live in hot, dry deserts.

camera

A **camera** is an instrument for taking photographs.

13

A B **C** D E F G H I J K L M N O P Q R S T U V W X Y Z

camp

To **camp** is to live outside. A **campsite** is a place where you set up your camping equipment.

can

A **can** is a sealed, metal container for storing food.

candle

A **candle** is a round stick of wax with a string through the middle. When you burn a candle, it gives off a bright light.

canoe

A **canoe** is a long, narrow boat that is moved through water with a paddle.

cap

A **cap** is a soft hat with a peak at the front.

car

A **car** is a vehicle with four wheels and an engine. You travel in a car from one place to another. A **carpark** is a place where a lot of cars can park.

carnation

A **carnation** is a flower with a sweet smell and a lot of petals.

carpenter

A **carpenter** is a person who builds things out of wood. Some carpenters help to build houses. Other carpenters make furniture.

carrot

A **carrot** is a long vegetable that grows underground.

carry

To **carry** something is to take it from one place to another.

cassette

A **cassette** is a plastic container that stores sounds, like music, on special tape. You use a **cassette player** to listen to a cassette.

castle

A **castle** is a large building with thick, stone walls and tall towers. Castles were built hundreds of years ago to keep people safe from their enemies. Kings and queens lived in castles.

a b **c** d e f g h i j k l m n o p q r s t u v w x y z

cat

A **cat** is a furry animal that is often kept as a pet.

catch

To **catch** is to grab hold of something as it comes towards you.

caterpillar

A **caterpillar** is a hairy insect with a long body.

cauliflower

A **cauliflower** is a vegetable with green leaves and a white centre.

cave

A **cave** is a large, dark hole in the side of a rock or under the ground.

centipede

A **centipede** is a tiny animal with many pairs of legs.

cereal

rye   oats   wheat   barley

Cereal is a kind of grass that is grown for its seeds. The seeds are used to make food like flour or breakfast cereal.

chair

A **chair** is a piece of furniture for one person to sit on.

chameleon

A **chameleon** is a type of lizard. It can change the colour of its skin to match the leaves and branches it is sitting on.

champion

A **champion** is a person who wins a sporting event or competition.

chase

To **chase** is to run after someone.

cheap

When something is **cheap**, you can buy it with a small amount of money.

A B **C** D E F G H I J K L M N O P Q R S T U V W X Y Z

checkout

A **checkout** is a cash-desk in a supermarket. Customers go through the checkout to pay for what they want to buy.

cheer

To **cheer** is to shout and wave your hands in the air with excitement.

cheese

Cheese is a food made from milk.

chess

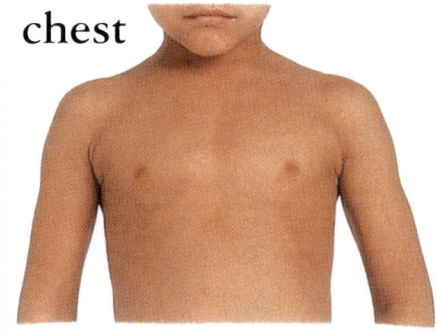

Chess is a game played on a chessboard.

chest

Your **chest** is the front part of your body, between your neck and your stomach.

chicken

cockerel

hen

chick

A **chicken** is a type of farm bird. A female chicken is called a **hen**. A male chicken is called a **cockerel**. A baby chicken is called a **chick**.

child

A **child** is a young boy or girl. **Children** grow up to become adults.

chimney

A **chimney** is a long pipe on top of a building. It takes away the smoke from a fire.

chimpanzee

A **chimpanzee** is a kind of ape. Chimpanzees live in family groups and play games together.

cheetah

A **cheetah** is a large, wild cat with a spotted coat. A cheetah can run faster than any other animal in the world.

a **b** c d e f g h i j k l m n o p q r s t u v w x y z

chin

Your **chin** is the part of your face below your mouth.

chocolate

Chocolate is a sweet bar made from cocoa and sugar.

choir

A **choir** is a group of people who sing together.

choose

To **choose** is to pick one thing instead of another.

chop-sticks
Chop-sticks are two thin sticks that you use to pick up and eat food.

church
A **church** is a building where Christian people meet to pray and to sing hymns.

circle
A **circle** is a type of shape. Circles are round.

city
A **city** is a large, important town with lots of buildings where people live and work.

clap

To **clap** is to bring your hands together and make a loud noise.

claw

A **claw** is the sharp, hooked nail on the foot of a bird or an animal.

clean
When something is **clean**, it is not dirty. One boot is clean, but the other is covered in mud.
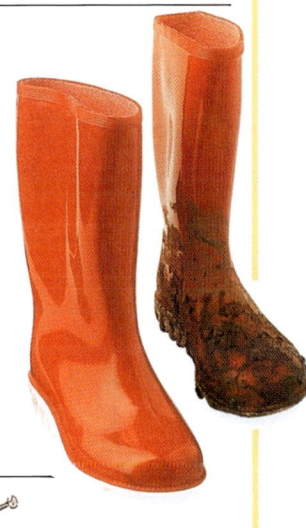

17

A B **C** D E F G H I J K L M N O P Q R S T U V W X Y Z

cliff
A **cliff** is a high, steep rock near the sea. Waves crash against the cliffs.

cloud
A **cloud** is made out of drops of water floating in the sky.

clown
A **clown** is a funny person who makes people laugh. Clowns wear colourful clothes and paint their faces.

coconut

A **coconut** is a fruit with a hard shell outside and coconut milk inside. Coconuts grow on coconut palms.

coffee

Coffee is a drink made from the brown seeds of the coffee bush. The seeds are called beans and are roasted and crushed to make a powder.

climb
To **climb** is to go to the top of something using your hands and feet.

coat

A **coat** is an item of clothing that you wear outside to keep yourself warm.

cold
When something is **cold**, it is not hot. When the weather is cold you may feel chilly and wear a coat.

clock

A **clock** is a machine that shows you the time.

cobweb
A **cobweb** is a net made by a spider to catch flies.

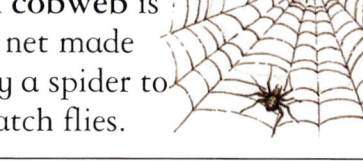

cockpit
A **cockpit** is the part of an aeroplane where the pilot sits. All the controls for flying the aeroplane are in the cockpit.

colour
Red, blue, and yellow are **colours**. All other colours are a mixture of these colours.

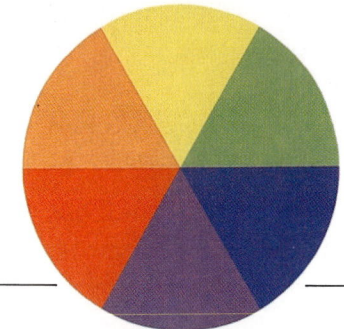

clothes

Clothes are the things that people wear. Clothes are usually made from cloth.

18

a b **c** d e f g h i j k l m n o p q r s t u v w x y z

compact disc
A **compact disc** is a flat circle of plastic that stores sounds and pictures. Two types include musical CDs and CD-ROMs for computers.

continent
A **continent** is a large piece of land. We divide the world into seven continents: 1 Africa, 2 Antarctica, 3 Asia, 4 Australasia, 5 Europe, 6 North America, 7 South America.

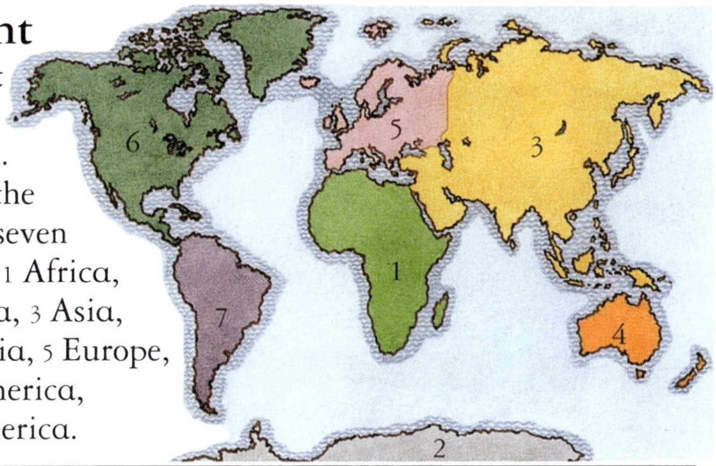

computer

A **computer** is a machine that people use to write, to work with numbers, and to store information. You use a keyboard to call up the information on the screen.

cook
To **cook** is to heat food and get it ready to eat.

corner
A **corner** is the point where two lines meet. This shape has four corners.

country
A **country** is a large area of land that is surrounded by borders and has its own laws. France is a country.

conductor

A **conductor** is a person who keeps an orchestra playing together.

cotton
Cotton is the white fibre that grows on a cotton-plant. Cotton is woven into cloth.

cousin

cone
A **cone** is a solid shape that is round at one end and pointed at the other.

count
To **count** is to say numbers one after the other.

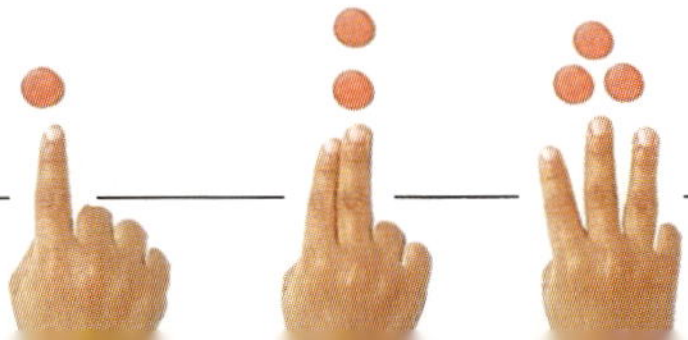

A **cousin** is a child of your aunt or uncle. An **aunt** is a sister of your mother or father. An **uncle** is a brother of your mother or father.

A B C D E F G H I J K L M N O P Q R S T U V W X Y Z

cow

cow
calf

A **cow** is a large, farm animal that gives us milk to drink. Cows are female **cattle**. Male cattle are called **bulls** and young cattle are called **calves**.

crab

A **crab** is a sea animal with two claws and eight legs. Crabs have a hard shell to protect their soft bodies.

crane

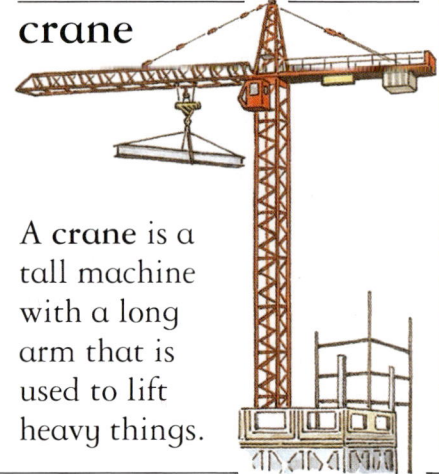

A **crane** is a tall machine with a long arm that is used to lift heavy things.

crawl

To **crawl** is to move along on your hands and knees.

crayon

A **crayon** is a coloured pencil that you use for drawing.

cricket

Cricket is a team game that is played with a cricket bat and ball.

cricket

A **cricket** is a small insect that chirps by rubbing its legs together.

crocodile

A **crocodile** is an animal with large jaws and a powerful tail that helps it to swim.

crow

A **crow** is a type of bird. It has black feathers and a large, black beak.

crowd

A **crowd** is a large number of people squashed together in one place.

crown

A **crown** is a ring of gold and jewels that is worn on the head. Kings and queens wear crowns.

a b c d e f g h i j k l m n o p q r s t u v w x y z

crutch
A **crutch** is a long, metal stick that helps you walk.

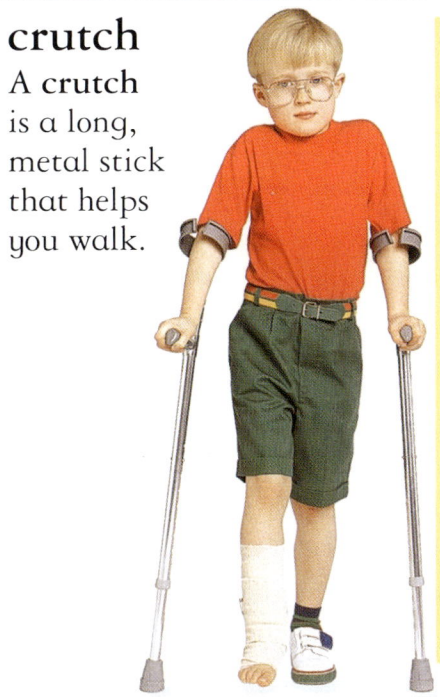

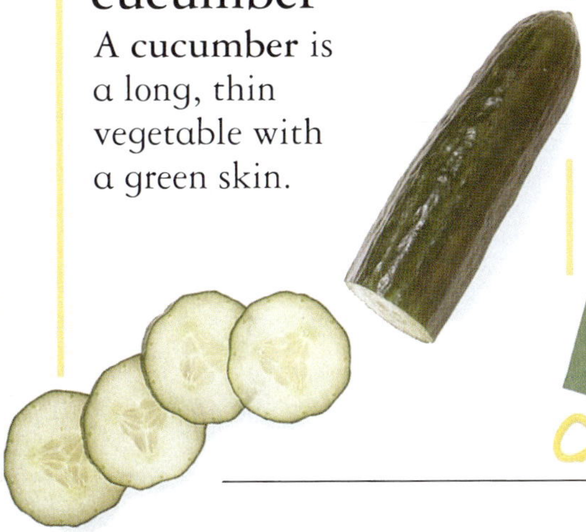

cup
A **cup** is a container that you drink out of.

cupboard

A **cupboard** is a piece of furniture with doors on the front. You store things on shelves in a cupboard.

cry

When you **cry**, tears run down your face. Crying shows that you are sad or hurt.

curtain
A **curtain** is a piece of material that hangs over or around a window. The curtain can be pulled across to cover the window.

cube
A **cube** is a solid shape with six square sides.

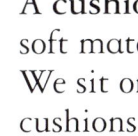

cushion
A **cushion** is a bag full of soft material or feathers. We sit on cushions.

cucumber
A **cucumber** is a long, thin vegetable with a green skin.

cut

To **cut** something is to slice it into pieces.

D

Dd *Dd* Dd *Dd*

daffodil

A **daffodil** is a yellow spring flower that grows from a bulb.

daisy

A **daisy** is a flower with white petals and a yellow centre.

dam
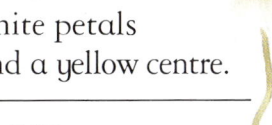

A **dam** is a strong wall built across a river. A dam holds back water to make a lake.

21

A B C D E F G H I J K L M N O P Q R S T U V W X Y Z

dance

To **dance** is to move your body in time to music.

deer
A **deer** is a large, shy animal that can run very fast. A female deer is called a **doe**, and a young deer is called a **fawn**. Male deer are called **stags** and have antlers.

dandelion
A **dandelion** is a yellow wild flower.

day
A **day** is 24 hours long. **Morning, afternoon, evening,** and **night** are all parts of one day.

morning

evening

afternoon

night

dentist
A **dentist** is a person who takes care of your teeth.
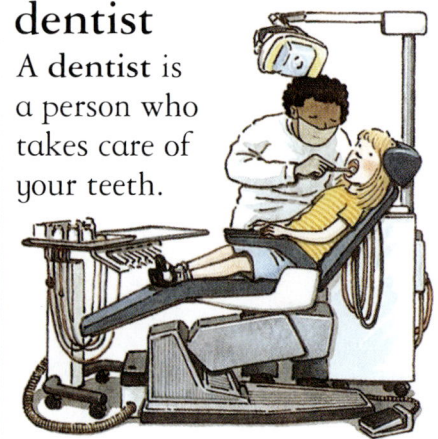

dessert
A **dessert** is a sweet food that you eat at the end of a meal.

desert
A **desert** is a hot, dry, and sandy area of land.

detective
A **detective** is someone who hunts for clues and solves crimes.

deaf
To be **deaf** is to have difficulty hearing. Some deaf people use sign language to talk to each other.

desk
A **desk** is a type of table that you sit at to read and write.

diagram
A **diagram** is a detailed drawing that explains how things work.
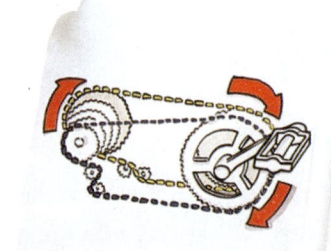

diamond
A **diamond** is a precious stone that sparkles. It is clear like glass.

diary
A **diary** is a small notebook in which you write what has happened in your day.

dictionary
A **dictionary** is a book with a list of words and their meanings arranged in alphabetical order. This book is a dictionary.

different
When two things are **different**, they are not the same.

dinner
Dinner is the main meal of the day.

dinosaur
A **dinosaur** is a huge animal that lived millions of years ago. Dinosaurs are now extinct.

dirty
When something is **dirty**, it is not clean. The dirty shoe is the one that is covered in mud.

disguise
A **disguise** is something you wear to hide who you are. Disguises make you look like someone else.

dive
To **dive** is to jump head first into water. A **diver** is a person who can dive.

doctor
A **doctor** is a person who helps sick or injured people to get well.
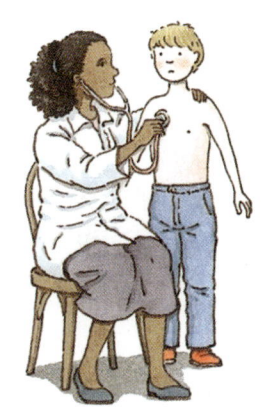

dog
A **dog** is a furry animal with a tail that wags. Dogs are often kept as pets.
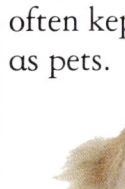

doll
A **doll** is a type of toy. Dolls look like babies or miniature people.

A B C **D** E F G H I J K L M N O P Q R S T U V W X Y Z

dolphin

A **dolphin** is an animal that lives in the sea. Dolphins are friendly and intelligent animals.

donkey

A **donkey** is an animal that looks like a small horse. Donkeys have long ears and a cross of fur on their backs.

door

A **door** is an entrance into a house or a room.

double

When something is **double**, it is twice as big or twice as many.

down

To move **down** is to go to a lower place. This train is travelling across the bridge and down the hill.

dragon

A **dragon** is an imaginary animal. Dragons have wings and they breathe fire.

dragonfly

A **dragonfly** is a flying insect with a long, thin body and four wings.

draw

To **draw** is to make lines that form a picture.

drawer

A **drawer** is a box that slides in and out of a **chest of drawers**.

dress

A **dress** is a garment worn by girls and women. The top and the skirt are joined together to make one piece.

dress

To **dress** yourself is to put on your clothes.

drill

A **drill** is a tool for making holes in wood, stone, or metal.

24

a b c d e f g h i j k l m n o p q r s t u v w x y z

drink
To **drink** is to swallow a liquid such as juice or water.

drive
To **drive** a vehicle is to operate and steer it.
A **driver** is a person who can drive a vehicle.

drop
To **drop** something is to let it fall to the ground.

drum
A **drum** is a musical instrument that you play by tapping it with **drumsticks**.

dry

To **dry** your body is to rub away water with a towel.

duck

drake

duck

duckling

A **duck** is a type of bird that swims on water. Ducks have webbed feet and a flat beak. A male duck is called a **drake** and a baby duck is called a **duckling**.

dumper truck

A **dumper truck** is a lorry that is used to carry heavy loads of sand, soil, and stones.

E

Ee *Ee* Ee *Ee*

eagle
An **eagle** is a large, powerful bird of prey.

ear
Your **ear** is a part of your head. You have two ears for hearing.

Earth
The **Earth** is the planet on which we live. The Earth is our world.

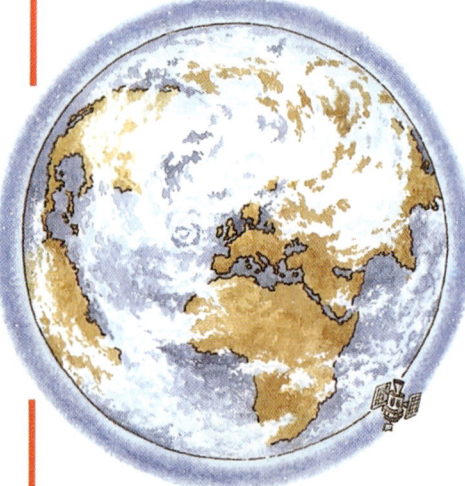

easel
An **easel** is a stand for holding a picture whilst you paint it.

eat
To **eat** is to put food into your mouth, chew it, and swallow it.

egg
An **egg** is an unborn baby animal. Birds, insects, fish, and reptiles lay eggs. When an egg hatches, a baby animal comes out.

eight
Eight is the number that comes after seven and before nine.

elbow
Your **elbow** is the middle joint in your arm.

elbow

electricity
Electricity is a powerful force. Electricity makes machines work and gives us light and heat.

elephant
An **elephant** is a huge, grey animal with a long trunk, large floppy ears, and two tusks.

empty
Something that is **empty** has nothing in it.

emu
An **emu** is a large bird with long legs. Emus cannot fly, but they can run very fast.

engine

An **engine** is a machine that makes things move or run. All cars have engines.

a b c d **e** f g h i j k l m n o p q r s t u v w x y z

engineer

An **engineer** is someone who builds and mends engines and machinery. Some engineers build bridges and buildings.

exit

The **exit** is the way out of a building.

enter

To **enter** a building is to go into it through an **entrance**.

equator

The **equator** is an imaginary line around the Earth, halfway between the North and South Poles.

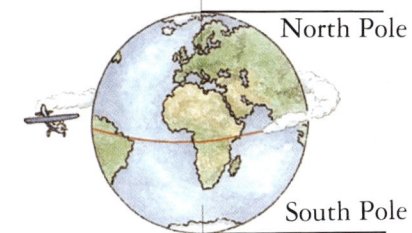

expensive

When something is **expensive**, it costs a lot of money to buy.

envelope

An **envelope** is a paper covering for a **letter**.

escalator

An **escalator** is a moving staircase.

explode

When something **explodes**, it blows up and makes a loud noise.

equal

When things are **equal**, they are the same size, number, or weight as each other. These scales show that the red apples and green apples are equal in weight.

exercise

To **exercise** is to make your body stronger and fitter. This boy is exercising his chest and arms.

eye

Your **eyes** are a part of your face. You have two eyes for seeing.

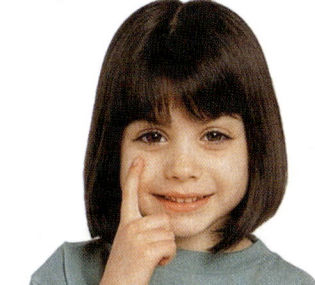

A B C D E F G H I J K L M N O P Q R S T U V W X Y Z

F

Ff *Ff* Ff *Ff*

face
Your **face** is the front part of your head. Your eyes, nose, and mouth are parts of your face.

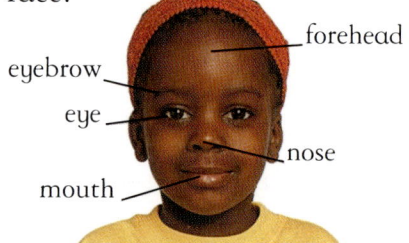
- forehead
- eyebrow
- eye
- nose
- mouth

factory
A **factory** is a building where a lot of people work together to make something.

fall
To **fall** is to drop to the ground.

family
A **family** is a group of people who are related to each other. A **mother**, a **father**, a **brother**, and a **sister** are just one kind of family.

fan
A **fan** is a folded piece of paper that you wave to make a breeze.

farm
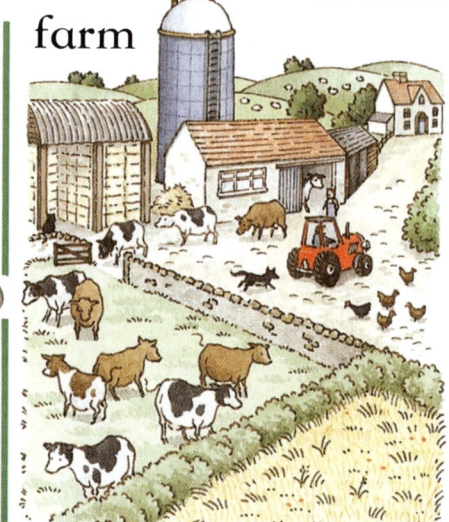

A **farm** is a piece of land for growing crops and keeping animals. A **farmer** is a person who works on a farm.

fast
When something moves **fast**, it moves very quickly. This top is spinning fast.

fat
When something is **fat**, it is not thin. One of these hamsters looks fat because its cheeks are packed with nuts.

feather
A **feather** is one of the light parts that covers a bird.

fair
A **fair** is a place where people go to have fun. You can ride on a merry-go-round or a big wheel, and play games at the side-shows.

28

a b c d e **f** g h i j k l m n o p q r s t u v w x y z

fight
To **fight** is to battle against someone or something.

film
A **film** is a thin strip of plastic that stores pictures. You can watch a film in a **cinema**.

finger
Your **finger** is a part of your hand. You have ten fingers.

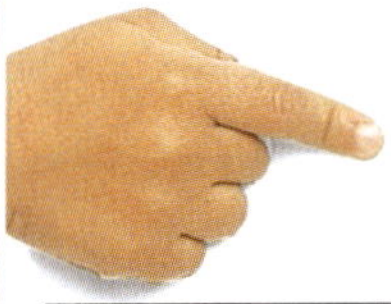

fingerprint
A **fingerprint** is the mark made when you press your finger on something.

finish
To **finish** is to reach the end of something.

fire
A **fire** is heat, flames, and light made by something burning.

fire engine
A **fire engine** is a large truck that carries **fire fighters**, hoses, and a water pump to a fire.

first-aid

First-aid is the help given to an injured person before a doctor arrives.

fish
A **fish** is a kind of animal that lives in water.

fish
To **fish** is to try to catch a fish.

five
Five is the number that comes after four and before six.

flag
A **flag** is a symbol of a country, a club, or a group of people. It is made from a large piece of cloth with a pattern on it.

flipper
A **flipper** is a kind of arm on a sea-lion or a penguin. Flippers are used for swimming or moving along on land.

flipper

29

A B C D E **F** G H I J K L M N O P Q R S T U V W X Y Z

float
When something **floats**, it stays on top of water.

flood
A **flood** is a great flow of water that goes over dry land.

flour
Flour is a powder made from grain. It is used to make bread and cakes.

flower
A **flower** is the colourful part of a plant or a tree. There are many different kinds of flowers.

flute
A **flute** is a long, thin musical instrument. You play a flute by blowing across a hole at one end and pressing the keys with your fingers.

fly
To **fly** is to move through the air like a bird, a kite, or an aeroplane.

fly
A **fly** is a small, flying insect with two wings and six legs.

fog
Fog is a thick, grey cloud that hangs close to the ground.

fold
To **fold** something is to bend one part over the other part.

food
Food is all the things that we eat. Food gives us energy and helps our bodies to grow bigger and stronger.

foot
Your **foot** is the part of your body at the end of your leg. You have two **feet**.

a b c d e **f** g h i j k l m n o p q r s t u v w x y z

football

American football

A **football** is a round or oval ball that is used to play a team game called **football**.

footprint
A **footprint** is the mark made by your shoe or foot on the ground.

forest
A **forest** is a large area of land where lots of trees grow.

fork
A **fork** is a tool that you use to pick up food.

fossil
A **fossil** is the remains of an animal or plant that lived millions of years ago. Fossils are found in rocks.

fountain
A **fountain** is a jet of water that shoots up into the air.

four
Four is the number that comes after three and before five.

fox
A **fox** is a wild animal that looks like a dog with a long, bushy tail.

friend
A **friend** is someone who you like a lot.

frog

A **frog** is an animal with webbed feet and strong back legs for jumping in and out of water.

fruit

A **fruit** is the juicy, seeded part of a plant.

A B C D E F G H I J K L M N O P Q R S T U V W X Y Z

frying-pan

A **frying-pan** is a wide, flat, metal cooking dish with a handle.

full
When something is **full**, it can hold no more.

fur
Fur is the thick, soft hair that grows on some animals and keeps them warm.

furniture

table
cupboard
bed
chair

Pieces of **furniture** are some of the moveable things in a house. Chairs and tables are pieces of furniture.

G

Gg Gg Gg Gg

game
A **game** is a competition with special rules.

garage
A **garage** is a building where cars are parked.

garden
A **garden** is a place where lots of colourful flowers and vegetables are grown.

gate
A **gate** is a door in a fence or a wall.

ghost
A **ghost** is the spirit of a dead person. This is a pretend ghost.

giant
A **giant** is a huge, imaginary person.

a b c d e f **g** h i j k l m n o p q r s t u v w x y z

giraffe

A **giraffe** is an animal with a very long neck and long, thin legs. Giraffes are the tallest animals in the world.

girl

A **girl** is a female child.

give

To **give** is to hand something to someone.

glass
Glass is a hard material that you can see through. It breaks easily.

glasses

Glasses are worn over your eyes if you need help to see better.

globe
A **globe** is a round ball with a map of the world printed on it.

glove

A **glove** is a warm covering for your hand.

glue
Glue is a paste that you use to stick things together.

goal
A **goal** is two posts with a net or an empty space between them. In some games you kick a ball between the posts to score a goal.

goat
A **goat** is an animal with a beard under its chin and short horns. A female goat is called a **nanny goat**. A male goat is called a **billy goat**, and a young goat is called a **kid**.

goggles
Goggles are special glasses that protect your eyes in the water.

gold
Gold is a precious, yellow metal that can be made into jewellery. Gold is found in rocks.

goldfish
A **goldfish** is a small, orange fish that is often kept as a pet.
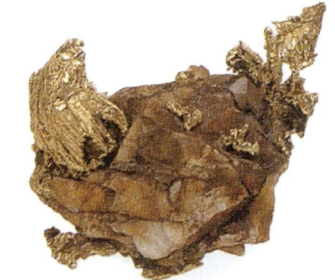

33

A B C D E F **G** H I J K L M N O P Q R S T U V W X Y Z

golf
Golf is an outdoor game that is played with golf clubs and a golf ball. You use a club to hit a ball into a hole in the ground.

goose
A **goose** is a water bird with a short beak and a long neck. Male **geese** are called **ganders** and young geese are called **goslings**.

gander

gosling

gorilla
A **gorilla** is a big, strong ape.

grandparent
A **grandparent** is the parent of your mother or your father. Here are a **grandmother**, a **grandfather**, and their **grandchildren**.

grape
A **grape** is a small, round fruit that grows in a bunch on a grapevine.

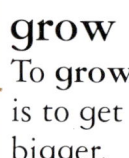

grapefruit
A **grapefruit** is a round fruit with yellow skin.

grass
Grass is a green plant that covers the ground.

grasshopper
A **grasshopper** is a jumping insect with long, strong legs.

green
Green is a colour. Leaves are green in the summer.

grow
To **grow** is to get bigger.

guitar
A **guitar** is a musical instrument with a long neck and strings. You play a guitar by strumming or plucking the strings.

gymnast
A **gymnast** is a person who does special exercises in a **gymnasium**.

a b c d e f g **h** i j k l m n o p q r s t u v w x y z

H

Hh *Hh* Hh Hh

hair
Hair is the soft covering that grows on your head and body.

half
A **half** is one of two equal parts. Two **halves** make a whole.

hammer
A **hammer** is a tool that you use for knocking in nails.

hand
Your **hand** is the part of your body below your wrist at the end of your arm. You hold things in your hand.

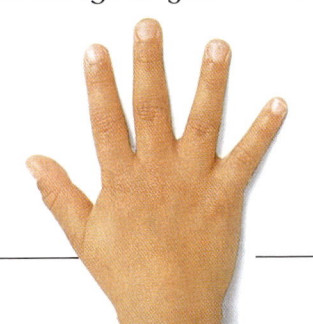

handle
A **handle** is the part of something that you hold.

hang
To **hang** something is to attach the top of it to a hook.

hangar
A **hangar** is a large building where aeroplanes are kept.

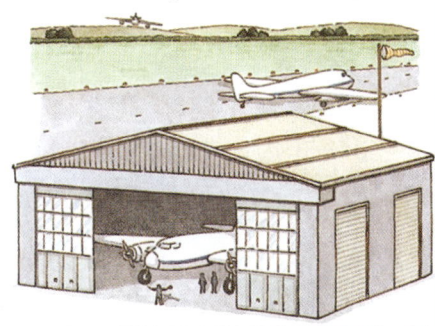

happy
A **happy** person is someone who feels pleased.

harbour
A **harbour** is a sheltered place, on a coast, where ships and boats are kept safely.

hat
A **hat** is a covering for your head.

hawk
A **hawk** is a bird of prey. Hawks eat small animals such as rabbits and fish.

head
Your **head** is the part of your body that is above your neck.

35

A B C D E F G **H** I J K L M N O P Q R S T U V W X Y Z

headlamp
A **headlamp** is the light on the front of a car or truck.

hearing-aid
A **hearing-aid** is a machine that you wear in your ear if you have difficulty hearing.

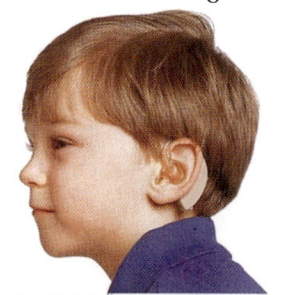

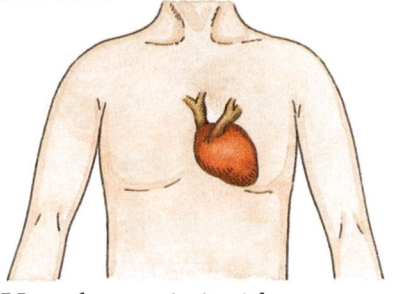

heart
Your **heart** is inside your chest. It pumps blood around your body.

heavy
If something is **heavy**, it weighs a lot and is difficult to move.

heel
Your **heel** is at the back of your foot.

ankle

heel

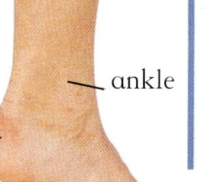

helicopter
A **helicopter** is a flying-machine that has large, spinning blades on top to lift it into the air.

helmet
A **helmet** is a hard hat that protects your head.

help
To **help** is to make someone's job easier.

hibernate
When an animal **hibernates**, it sleeps through the cold winter months. Dormice and squirrels hibernate.

hide
To **hide** is to put something in a place where no one can see it. This girl is hiding herself behind the easel.

high
When something is **high**, it is not low. This hot-air balloon is high in the sky.

36

a b c d e f g **h** i j k l m n o p q r s t u v w x y z

hill
A **hill** is a big hump in the land. Hills are smaller than mountains.

hip
Your **hip** is the bony part of your body that sticks out just below your **waist**. Your legs join your body at your hips.

hippopotamus
A **hippopotamus** is a large animal with very thick skin and short legs. It likes to wallow in muddy water.

hold
To **hold** something is to have it in your hands or arms.

hole
A **hole** is an opening in something.

honey
Honey is a sweet, sticky syrup that is made by bees.

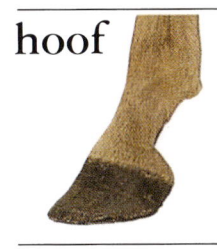

hoof
A **hoof** is the hard covering on the feet of some animals.

hop
To **hop** is to jump up and down on one leg.

horn
A **horn** is something that makes a loud noise to warn people of danger.

horse
A **horse** is a large animal with a mane, a tail, and hooves. A female horse is called a **mare**, a male horse is called a **stallion**, and a baby horse is called a **foal**.

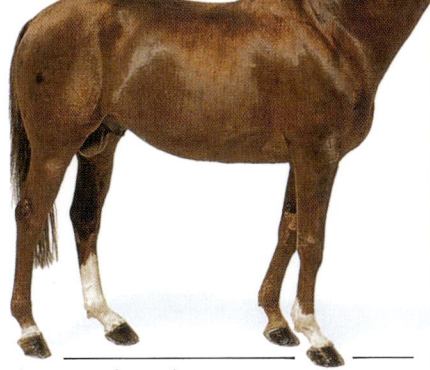

hospital
A **hospital** is a place where doctors and nurses take care of sick or injured people.

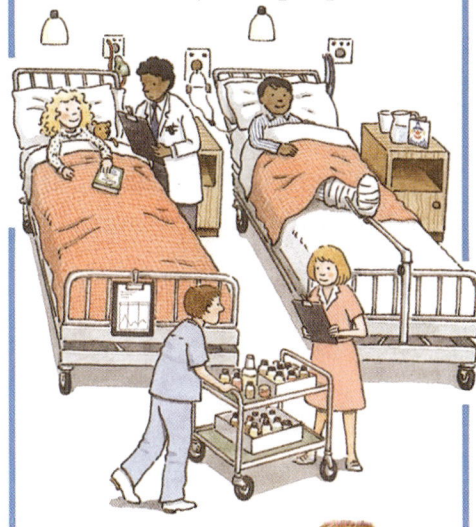

hot
When something is **hot**, it is not cold. When the weather is hot, the heat makes you feel very warm.

37

A B C D E F G H I J K L M N O P Q R S T U V W X Y Z

hotel
A **hotel** is a building with a lot of bedrooms. People pay to sleep and eat in a hotel.

I

Ii *Ii* Ii *Ii*

house
A **house** is a building where people live.

hutch
A **hutch** is a pet rabbit's house.

ice
Ice is frozen water.

iceberg
An **iceberg** is a very large piece of ice that floats in the ocean.

hug
To **hug** is to put your arms around something and hold it tightly.

hyena
A **hyena** is a wild animal that looks like a wolf. A hyena's call sounds like a loud, human laugh.

hundred
A **hundred** is the number that comes after 99 and before 101.

ice-cream
Ice-cream is a frozen dessert made from cream and eggs.

100

38

a b c d e f g h **i** j k l m n o p q r s t u v w x y z

icicle
An **icicle** is a hanging piece of ice made by water freezing as it drips.

igloo
An **igloo** is a house made from blocks of snow and ice.

iguana
An **iguana** is a large lizard with a long tail and a ridge of spines along its back. Iguanas live in trees.

injection
An **injection** is a special way that a doctor or nurse can give you medicine quickly. A needle is pricked into your skin, and the medicine is pushed through the needle into your body.

injure
To **injure** yourself is to hurt yourself. This boy has had an accident. He has an **injury** to his ankle and he's in a lot of pain.

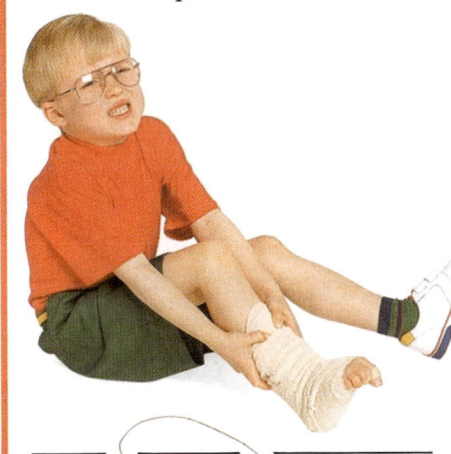

insect
An **insect** is a tiny animal with six legs, wings, and a body in three parts.

inside
When something is **inside**, it is within and not outside. These shoes are inside a shoebox.

instrument
An **instrument** is something that makes musical sounds.

tuba

invent
To **invent** is to make something that did not exist before. An **inventor** invents things.

invite
To **invite** someone is to ask them to a party or another event. A **invitation** is the card that you send.

iron
An **iron** is a hot tool that takes the creases out of clothes.

island
An **island** is a piece of land with water all around it.

ivy
Ivy is a plant that grows up walls and trees.

A B C D E F G H I **J** K L M N O P Q R S T U V W X Y Z

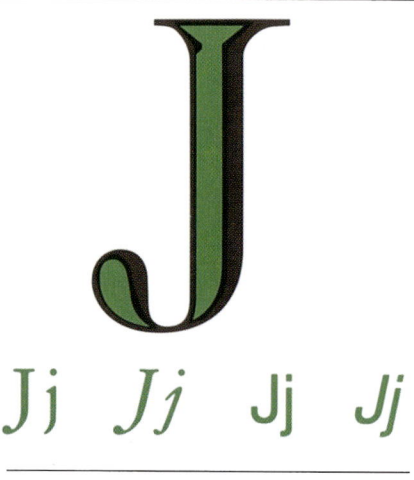

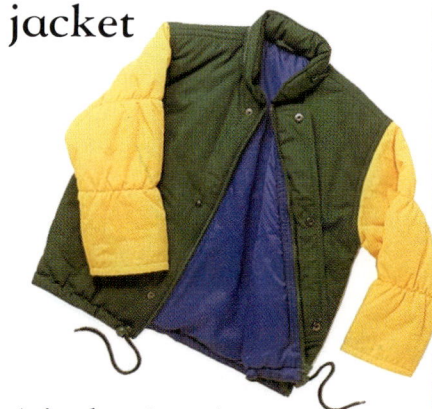

J

Jj *Jj* Jj *Jj*

jacket
A **jacket** is a short coat.

jaguar
A **jaguar** is a large, wild cat with a spotted coat.

jam
Jam is a sweet food that you spread on bread. It is made by boiling fruit with sugar.

jar
A **jar** is a glass container with a wide neck and a lid.

jaw
Your **jaw** is the bony part of your mouth that holds your teeth. You move your lower jaw when you chew.

jeans
Jeans are trousers made out of strong, blue cotton cloth.

jellyfish
A **jellyfish** is a sea animal with a soft body and long tentacles.

jewel
A **jewel** is a precious stone, like an emerald or a ruby. Jewels are used to make sparkling **jewellery** like these earrings.

jigsaw puzzle
A **jigsaw puzzle** is a picture cut up into pieces that you have to fit together again.

judo
Judo is a fighting sport using holds and throws.

jug
A **jug** is a container with a handle and a spout for pouring liquids.

a b c d e f g h i j k l m n o p q r s t u v w x y z

K
Kk *Kk* Kk *Kk*

juggle
To **juggle** is to keep several objects in the air by throwing and catching them quickly. A **juggler** is a person who can juggle.

juice
Juice is the liquid that comes out of fruit.

jump
To **jump** is to leap into the air so that both feet leave the ground.

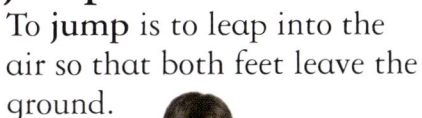

jungle
A **jungle** is a hot, steamy forest where it rains a lot. There are lots of tall trees in a jungle. Jungles can be called **rainforests**.

kangaroo
A **kangaroo** is an animal with long, powerful back legs, which it uses for jumping. A female kangaroo carries her baby in her pouch.

karat
Karate is a fighting sport using foot kicks and hand chops.

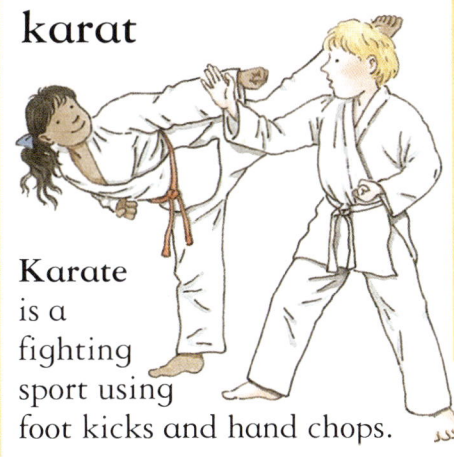

kennel
A **kennel** is a house for a pet dog.

key
A **key** is a metal tool for locking or unlocking doors.

kick
To **kick** is to hit out with your foot.

king
A **king** is a man who heads a country. Kings live in palaces.

kiss
To **kiss** is to touch someone with your lips.

41

A B C D E F G H I J **K** L M N O P Q R S T U V W X Y Z

kitchen
A **kitchen** is the room where food is cooked.

knit
To **knit** is to knot wool to make a sweater or a scarf. You knit with knitting-needles.

kite
A **kite** is a toy that you fly in the wind.

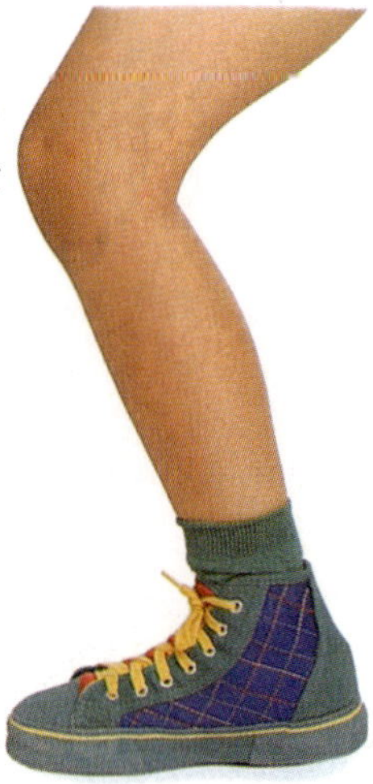

kneel
To **kneel** is to go down on your knees.

knock
To **knock** is to tap something with your knuckles to make a noise.

kitten
A **kitten** is a young cat.

knife
A **knife** is a tool with a sharp blade used for cutting.

knot
A **knot** is a fastening made by tying things together. This is a knot in a piece of rope.

knee
Your **knee** is the joint in the middle of your leg. Your leg bends at your knee.

knight
A **knight** is a brave soldier who lived hundreds of years ago. Knights wore suits of armour.

koala
A **koala** is a furry animal with big ears and a black nose. Koalas eat eucalyptus leaves and live in trees.

a b c d e f g h i j k **l** m n o p q r s t u v w x y z

L

Ll *Ll* Ll *Ll*

laboratory
A **laboratory** is a place where people learn about science, and do experiments.

ladder
A **ladder** is a tall climbing frame with lots of steps. You climb ladders to reach high places.

ladybird
A **ladybird** is a tiny insect that often has spotted wing cases.

lake
A **lake** is a large area of water surrounded by land.

lamb
A **lamb** is a young sheep.

lamp
A **lamp** is a stand for a bulb that is covered by a lampshade. A lamp gives out light.

land
Land is the part of the Earth that is not sea. We walk on land.

large
When something is **large**, it is not little. This large doll contains all the little dolls.

laugh
To **laugh** is to make sounds that show you are happy.

lawn
A **lawn** is a piece of ground that is covered with grass. A lawn is cut with a **lawnmower**.

leaf
A **leaf** is a flat, green part of a plant that grows from its stem.

43

A B C D E F G H I J K **L** M N O P Q R S T U V W X Y Z

lean

To **lean** is to tilt your body to one side.

leopard

A **leopard** is a wild cat with sharp teeth and claws. Leopards have a yellow coat with black spots.

lick

To **lick** something is to touch it with your tongue.

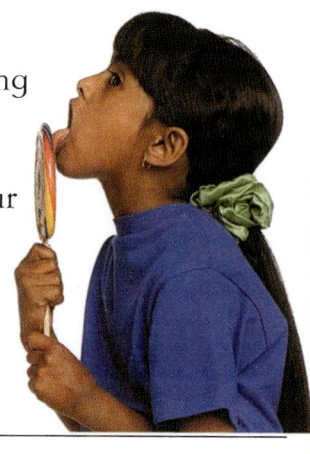

left

Left is the opposite of right. This girl is about to make a left turn on her bicycle.

letter

A **letter** is a part of the alphabet. You put letters together to make words.

lifeboat

A **lifeboat** is a type of boat that is used to rescue people out at sea.

leg

Your **leg** is the part of your body between your bottom and your foot. People walk on two legs.

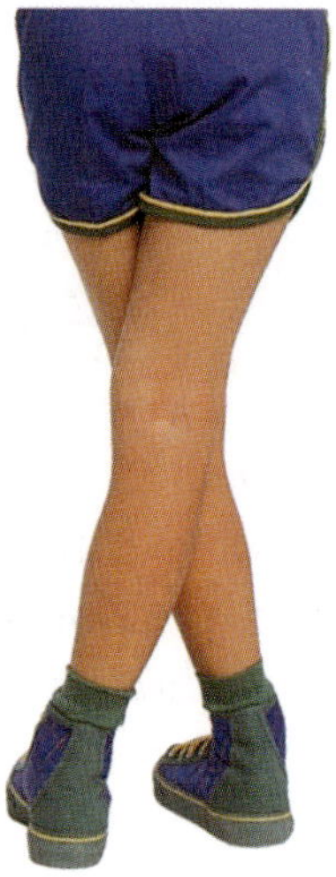

lettuce

Lettuce is a leafy, green vegetable that you eat in a salad.

lift

To **lift** something is to pick it up.

lemon

A **lemon** is a yellow fruit with a very sour taste.

library

A **library** is a place where lots of books are kept on shelves. You can borrow books to read from some libraries.

a b c d e f g h i j k **l** m n o p q r s t u v w x y z

light
If something is **light**, it is not heavy. Light things weigh very little and are easy to lift.

lighthouse
A **lighthouse** is a tall tower by the sea with a bright light on the top. Lighthouses warn ships of danger.

lightning
Lightning is a flash of light that appears in the sky during a **thunderstorm**.

lion
A **lion** is a fierce big cat that roars. A male lion has a shaggy mane around its head. A female lion is called a **lioness**.

lioness

lion

lip
Your **lips** are the soft, fleshy edges around your mouth.

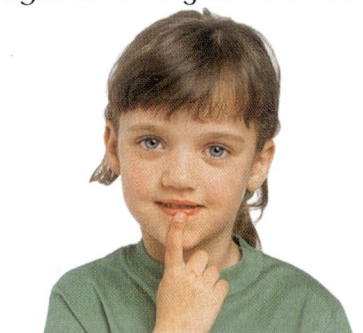

liquid
A **liquid** is wet and can be poured like this water.

litter
Litter is the wastepaper and other rubbish that should be put in a wastepaper-basket.

little
When something is **little**, it is not large. Little things are small in size like this purple flower. 

lizard
A **lizard** is a reptile with a long, scaly body, a tail, and four short legs.

lobster
A **lobster** is a sea animal with a hard shell, ten legs, and large claws.

lock
A **lock** is a fastening that you open with a key. This is a padlock.

log
A **log** is a thick piece of wood that has been cut from a tree.

45

A B C D E F G H I J K L M N O P Q R S T U V W X Y Z

long
When something is **long**, it measures a lot from end to end. One of these strings of beads is much longer than the other.

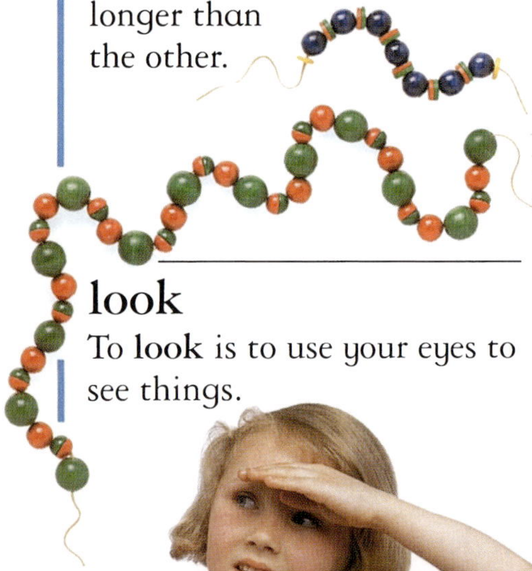

low
When something is **low**, it is not high. This girl is low down in the grass.

M

MmMmMmMm

look
To **look** is to use your eyes to see things.

luggage
Luggage is all the bags and cases that you take on holiday.

machine
A **machine** is an object with parts that move together to make something work. Clocks, cars, bicycles, and computers are all machines.

lose
When you **lose** something, you cannot find it. This girl has lost a shoe.

lunch
Lunch is the meal that you eat in the middle of the day.

magazine
A **magazine** is a thin book that you buy each week or month.

love
To **love** is to like someone or something very much.

lung
Your **lung** is inside your chest. You have two lungs for breathing.

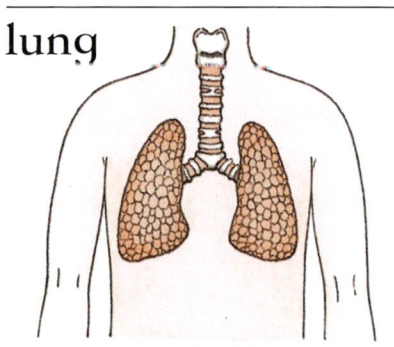

magic
Magic is a way of doing amazing tricks that seem to be impossible. A **magician** is a person who can do magic tricks.

46

a b c d e f g h i j k l m n o p q r s t u v w x y z

magnet
A **magnet** is a piece of iron or steel that can pull other pieces of iron or steel towards it.

magnifying glass
A **magnifying glass** is a special piece of glass that makes things look bigger than they really are.

mammal
A **mammal** is any warm-blooded animal that feeds on its mother's milk.

man
A **man** is a grown-up boy.

map
A **map** is a drawing of part of the Earth's surface. This map of the world shows where the countries are.

market
A **market** is a place where people buy and sell things from stalls.

mask
A **mask** is a covering for your face. You wear a mask to disguise yourself.

match
A **match** is a short stick that makes a flame when you rub it on a rough surface.

mathematics
Mathematics is the study of numbers, shapes, and sizes.

meal
A **meal** is the food that you eat at one time.

measure
To **measure** something is to find out what size it is.

meat
Meat is the part of an animal that is eaten as food.

47

A B C D E F G H I J K L M N O P Q R S T U V W X Y Z

mechanic
A **mechanic** is a person who makes and repairs cars or other machines.

microscope
A **microscope** is an instrument that makes tiny things look bigger.

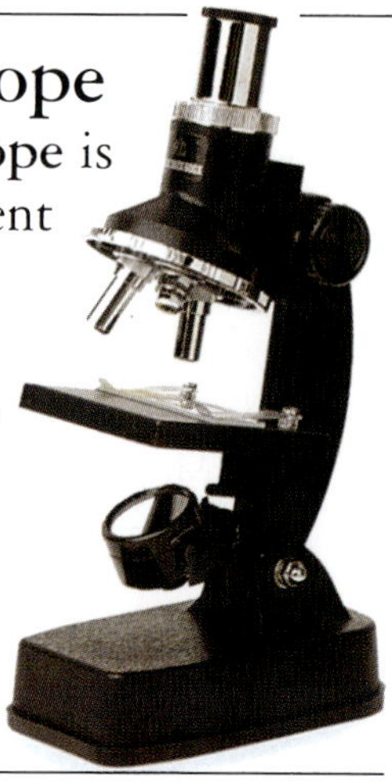

medal
A **medal** is a piece of metal, usually shaped like a large coin. Medals are given to people who win competitions.

melt
When something **melts**, it turns to liquid as it warms up.

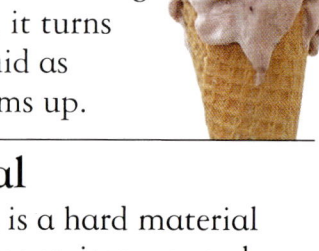

metal
Metal is a hard material like copper, iron, or steel. Metals are found in rocks.

microwave oven
A **microwave oven** is a machine for cooking food very quickly.

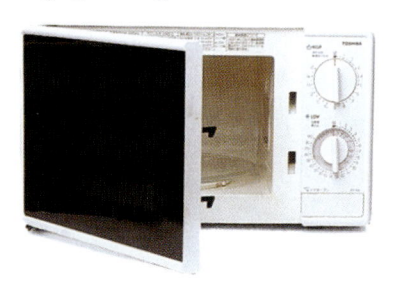

medicine
Medicine is a pill or a liquid that you take to make you better if you are ill. 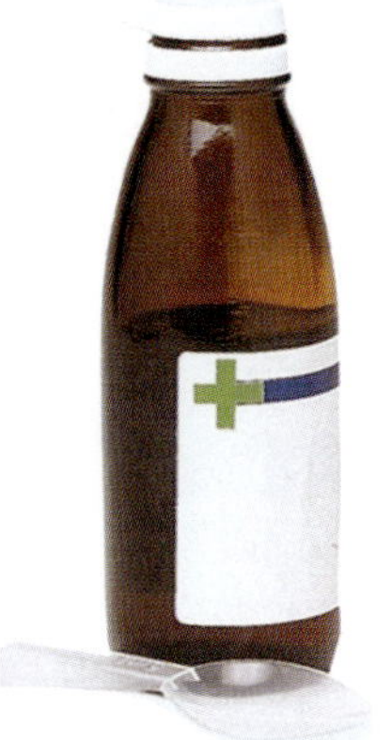

midday
Midday is the middle of the day. You eat your lunch at midday.

meet
To **meet** someone is to come face to face with them.

microphone
A **microphone** is an instrument that makes your voice sound louder.

midnight
Midnight is the middle of the night. You are asleep at midnight.

48

a b c d e f g h i j k l **m** n o p q r s t u v w x y z

milk
Milk is a white liquid that some animals make to feed their babies. Many people drink cow's milk.

mine
A **mine** is a deep hole under the ground where people dig for rocks like coal.

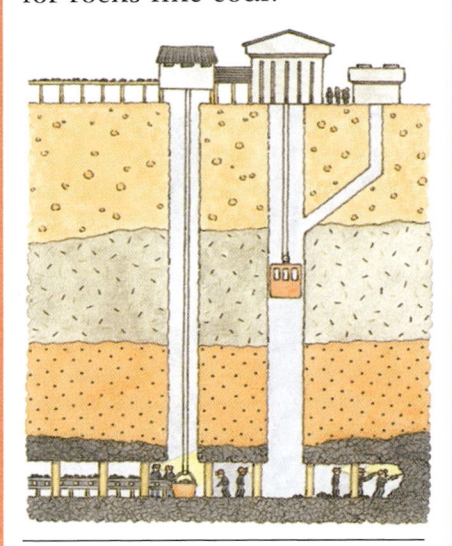

mineral
A **mineral** is a part of the rock that is dug out of a mine.

mirror
A **mirror** is a special piece of glass in which you can see your reflection.

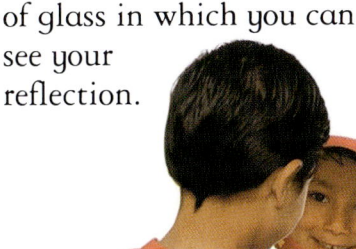

mix
To **mix** things is to stir them together.

money
Money is the coins and paper notes that we use to buy things.

monkey
A **monkey** is a furry animal with long arms, fingers, and toes. Monkeys have tails to help them to swing in trees.

monster
A **monster** is a strange, frightening creature that you read about in fairy tales.

month
A **month** is a measure of time that is about 30 days long. There are 12 months in a year.

January February April March May June July September August October November December

moon
The **moon** is the Earth's satellite. It shines in the sky at night.

mosaic
A **mosaic** is a picture made by fitting together coloured pieces of stone or glass.

49

A B C D E F G H I J K L **M** N O P Q R S T U V W X Y Z

mosque
A **mosque** is a building where Muslim people meet to pray.

mountain
A **mountain** is a very high, rocky hill.

mouth
Your **mouth** is part of your face. You use your mouth for eating and speaking.

mud
Mud is wet, soft earth.

mosquito
A **mosquito** is a flying insect that bites your skin to suck your blood.

muscle
Muscle is the part of your body that gives you strength to move and to lift things.

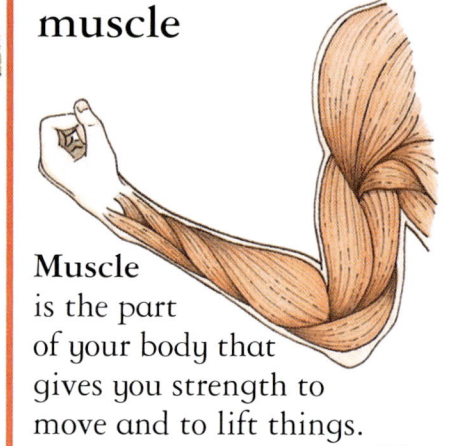

moth
A **moth** is an insect that looks like a butterfly. It flies around at night. 

mouse
A **mouse** is a small, furry animal with a long tail. **Mice** live in nests.

moustache
A **moustache** is the hair that grows above a man's lips.

museum
A **museum** is a building where you can see old and fascinating things.

motorcycle
A **motorcycle** is a machine that you ride. This motorcycle has a powerful engine.

N

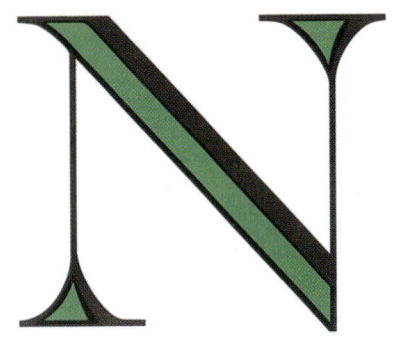

Nn *Nn* Nn *Nn*

mushroom
A **mushroom** is a fungus that is shaped like a small umbrella. You can eat some mushrooms, but others are poisonous.

music
Music is the notes that you read, or the sound that you make, when you are singing or playing an instrument.

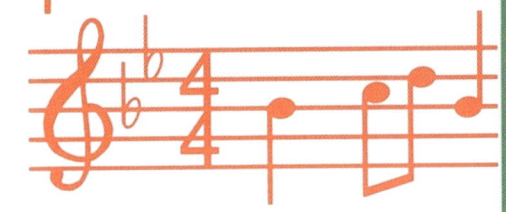

musician
A **musician** is a person who can make music by playing a musical instrument.

nail
A **nail** is a small, metal spike with a sharp point at one end. You hammer nails into wood.

narrow
When something is **narrow**, it is not wide. Narrow spaces are difficult to squeeze through.

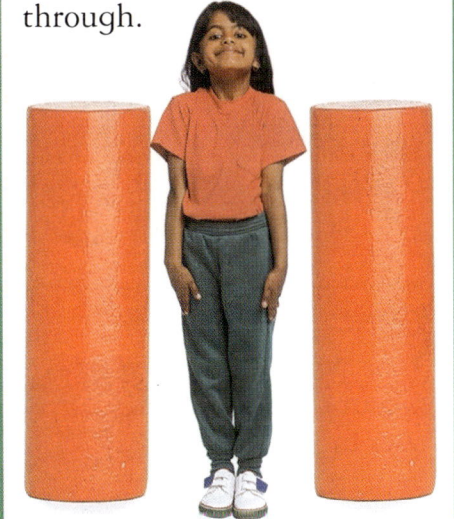

navy
A **navy** is a large group of warships carrying sailors who are trained to fight at sea in times of war.

neck
Your **neck** is the part of your body that is between your head and your shoulders.

needle
A **needle** is a thin, pointed piece of metal that you use for sewing.

nest
A **nest** is a home where an animal lives and cares for its babies.

net
Net is material made from loosely knotted string. You can catch fish in a net.

A B C D E F G H I J K L M **N** O P Q R S T U V W X Y Z

new
When something is **new**, it is not old. New things have just been made or bought.

newspaper
A **newspaper** is big sheets of paper with words printed on them. You read the newspapers to find out about world events.

newt
A **newt** is an animal that lives in or around water.

night
Night is the time when it is dark outside. Night begins at sunset and ends at sunrise.

nine
Nine is the number that comes after eight and before ten.

noise
A **noise** is a loud sound. This boy is making a noise, on his drum.

nose
Your **nose** is part of your face. You breathe through your nose.

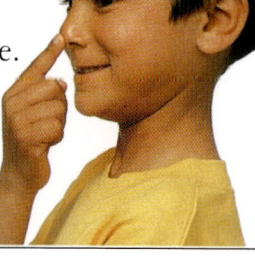

number
A **number** is a sign that tells you how many things there are.

nurse
A **nurse** is a person who is trained to take care of sick or injured people in a hospital.

nut
A **nut** is a small piece of metal that you screw on to a **bolt**. Nuts and bolts are used to hold things together.

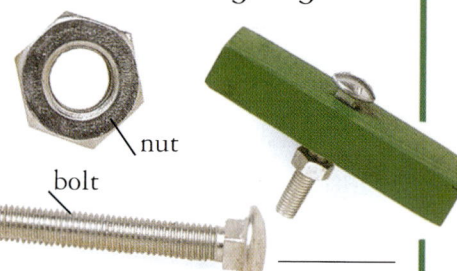

nut
A **nut** is a fruit with a hard shell and a soft inside that you can eat.

nutcracker
A **nutcracker** is a tool for breaking open nuts.

52

a b c d e f g h i j k l m n **o** p q r s t u v w x y z

O

Oo Oo Oo Oo

oar
An **oar** is a long pole with a flat blade at one end. You use oars to row a boat.

ocean
An **ocean** is a large body of salt water. The Pacific and the Atlantic are oceans.

octopus
An **octopus** is a sea animal with eight long arms and a soft, round body.

office
An **office** is a place where people go to work. There are desks, chairs, computers and filing cabinets in offices.

oil
Oil is a greasy liquid that makes machines run smoothly.

old
When something is **old**, it is not new. Old things look used.

one
One is the number that comes before two. When you count, you start with the number one.

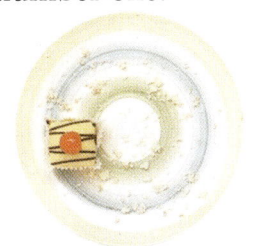

onion
An **onion** is a round vegetable that makes your eyes water when it's cut open.

open
When something is **open**, it is not shut or closed.

opera
An **opera** is a play in which the words are sung to music.

53

A B C D E F G H I J K L M N **O** P Q R S T U V W X Y Z

opposite
When things are the **opposite** of each other, they are completely different. Hot and cold are opposites, so are front and back.

orchard
An **orchard** is an area of land where fruit-trees are grown.

optician
An **optician** is a person who makes or sells glasses.

orchestra
An **orchestra** is a large group of musicians playing instruments together.

ostrich
An **ostrich** is a large bird with a long neck, long legs, and lots of big feathers. Ostriches cannot fly, but they can run very fast.

orange
Orange is a colour made by mixing red and yellow.

orange
An **orange** is a round, juicy fruit with a thick, orange-coloured skin.

organ
An **organ** is a musical instrument with a keyboard, and long metal pipes that make sounds when air is pushed through them.

otter
An **otter** is a furry animal that lives in or near water.

orangutan
An **orangutan** is a large ape with long fur, and strong arms.

outside
When something is **outside**, it is not inside. This puppy is outside its kennel.

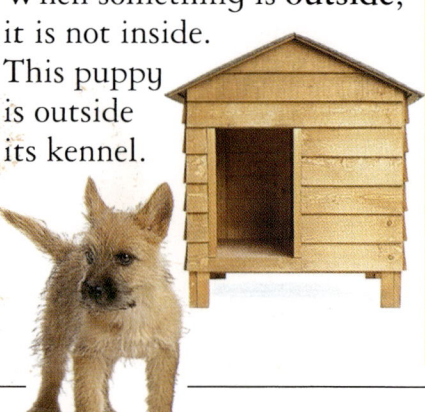

a b c d e f g h i j k l m n **o** p q r s t u v w x y z

oval
An **oval** is a type of shape. Eggs are oval.

oven
An **oven** is a machine for cooking food.

owl
An **owl** is a bird with a large head, and big, round eyes. Owls usually hunt for food at night.

oyster
An **oyster** is a sea animal with a soft body inside a hard shell. Some oysters make pearls inside their shells.

P

Pp *Pp* Pp *Pp*

page
A **page** is one side of a sheet of paper in a book.

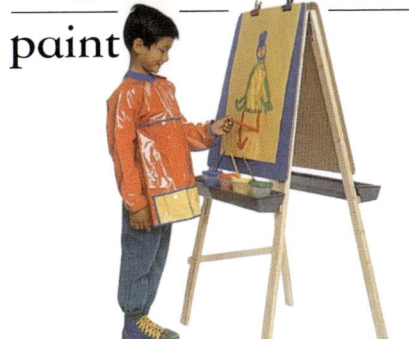

paint
To **paint** is to make a picture using a brush and paints.

paint
Paint is a coloured liquid used to paint pictures.

pair
A **pair** is a set of two things that are used together, like shoes or socks.

palace
A **palace** is a very large, grand house where kings and queens live.

palm
Your **palm** is the inside part of your hand.

palm tree
A **palm tree** is a tree that grows in hot countries. Palm trees have large leaves that grow at the top of a long trunk.

panda
A **panda** is a large, furry animal. Giant pandas look like bears with black and white fur.

55

A B C D E F G H I J K L M N O **P** Q R S T U V W X Y Z

panther
A **panther** is a large leopard with a black coat.

parent
A **parent** is a person who has a child. Your mother and father are your parents. You are their **son** or **daughter**.

passenger
A **passenger** is a person who travels in a bus or a car. Passengers do not do the driving.

paper
Paper is a material you use to write on.

park
A **park** is a piece of land where people can enjoy the gardens and playgrounds.

path
A **path** is a track for people to walk on.

parachute
A **parachute** is a large piece of material that is shaped like an umbrella. Parachutes help people to float through the air and land safely on the ground.

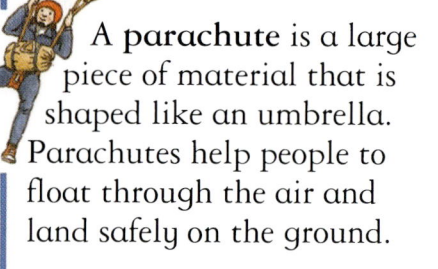

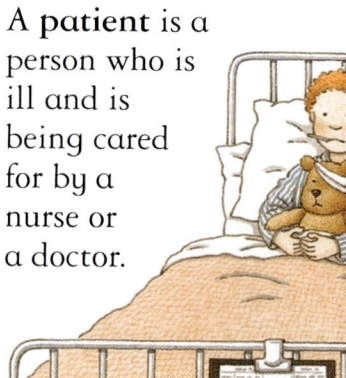

parrot
A **parrot** is a bird with brightly coloured feathers. Some parrots can be trained to repeat words.

patient
A **patient** is a person who is ill and is being cared for by a nurse or a doctor.

paw
A **paw** is an animal's foot.

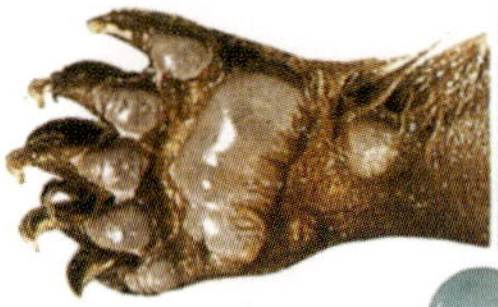

parcel
A **parcel** is something that is wrapped in paper.

party
A **party** is a group of friends having lots of fun together. You might have a party on your birthday.

a b c d e f g h i j k l m n o **p** q r s t u v w x y z

pay
To **pay** for something is to give money for it. The girl is paying the shopkeeper.

pea
A **pea** is a small, round vegetable that grows in a pod.

peach
A **peach** is a sweet, juicy fruit with a soft skin, and a stone in the middle.

peacock
A **peacock** is a bird with colourful tail feathers that open out like a fan.

peanut
A **peanut** is a seed that grows in a pod in the soil.

pear
A **pear** is a fruit that narrows at the top and has pips in the middle.

pearl
A **pearl** is a small, white gemstone that is found in some oyster shells. Pearls are used to make jewellery.

pebble
A **pebble** is a small, smooth stone found on the beach.

peel
Peel is the skin of some fruits and vegetables.

peel
To **peel** something is to take the skin off it. This girl is peeling an orange.

pelican
A **pelican** is a bird with a large pouch under its beak for catching fish to eat.

pen
A **pen** is a tool filled with ink used for writing.

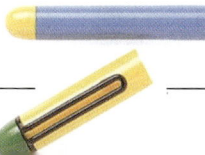

A B C D E F G H I J K L M N O **P** Q R S T U V W X Y Z

pencil
A **pencil** is a tool made from wood and lead. You use a pencil to write and to draw.

penguin
A **penguin** is a black and white sea bird that cannot fly. Penguins use their short wings to swim in the water.

people
People are **men**, **women**, and **children**.

pepper
Pepper is a powder made from the dried berries of a pepper plant. You use pepper to flavour food.

perfume
Perfume is a sweet-smelling liquid made from flower petals. You put perfume on your body.

pet
A **pet** is a tame animal that you take care of and keep at home as a friend.

petal
A **petal** is a coloured part of a flower.

photograph
A **photograph** is a picture taken with a camera.

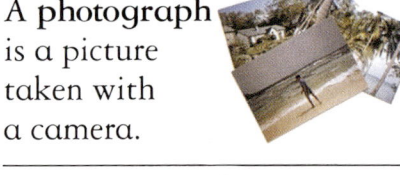

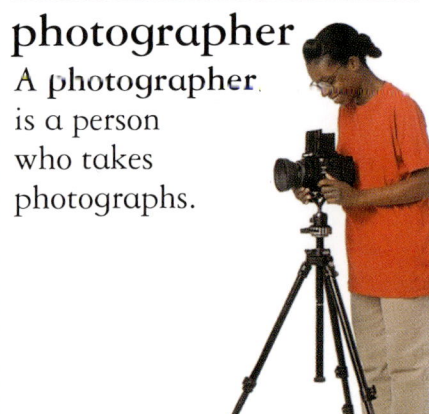

photographer
A **photographer** is a person who takes photographs.

piano
A **piano** is a large musical instrument with black and white keys. You press the keys to make music.

picnic
A **picnic** is a meal that you eat outside.

picture
When you make a **picture**, you draw or paint what something looks like.

pie
A **pie** is a pastry case filled with fruit, meat, or vegetables, and baked in an oven.

a b c d e f g h i j k l m n o **p** q r s t u v w x y z

pig

piglet

A **pig** is an animal with a short snout, a little tail, big ears, and bristly hairs on its skin. A male pig is called a **boar**. A female pig is called a **sow**, and a baby pig is called a **piglet**.

pigeon

A **pigeon** is a bird with a large, round body and a small head. Some pigeons live in cities.

pile

A **pile** is a lot of things stacked on top of one another.

pillow

A **pillow** is a bag of soft material for your head to rest on.

pilot

A **pilot** is a person who flies an aeroplane.

pin

A **pin** is a short, thin piece of metal used to hold cloth together.

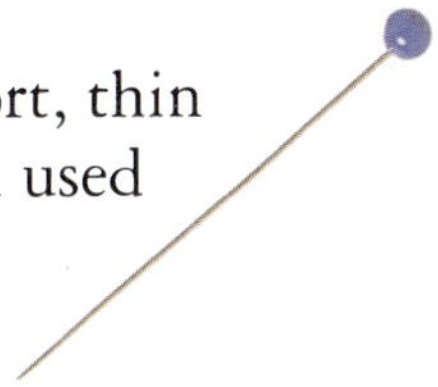

pineapple

A **pineapple** is a large fruit with thick, bumpy skin and pointed leaves. The fruit inside is sweet and juicy.

pink

Pink is a colour. It is made by mixing red and white.

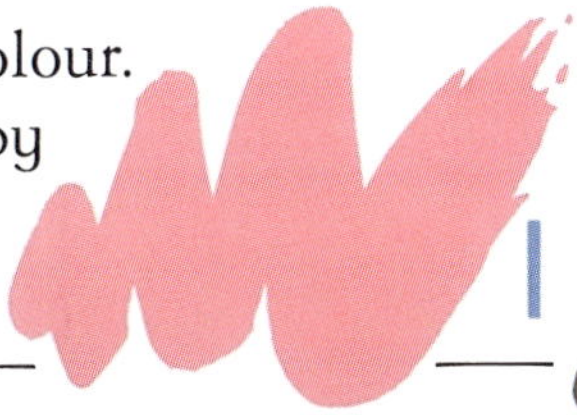

pipe

A **pipe** is a hollow tube of metal or plastic. Liquid runs through pipes.

pirate

A **pirate** is a robber who steals from ships at sea.

planet

A **planet** is a huge ball of rock, metal, and fire that moves around the sun. There are nine planets in space.

Pluto
Uranus
Neptune
Jupiter
Saturn
Mars
Earth
Mercury
Venus

59

A B C D E F G H I J K L M N O **P** Q R S T U V W X Y Z

plant
A **plant** is anything that grows in the soil. Flowers and trees are plants.

plastic
Plastic is a material made from chemicals. This blow-up toy is made out of plastic.

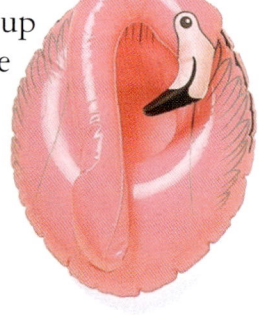

plate
A **plate** is a flat dish that you put food on.

play
To **play** is to have fun.

plum
A **plum** is a purple fruit with a stone in the middle.

plumber
A **plumber** is a person who works on water or gas pipes.

pocket
A **pocket** is a small bag that is sewn into your clothes.

point
A **point** is the sharp end of something. These objects all have sharp points.

polar bear
A **polar bear** is a huge bear covered in thick, white fur.

police officer
A **police officer** is a person who keeps law and order.

polish
To **polish** is to rub something to make it shine.

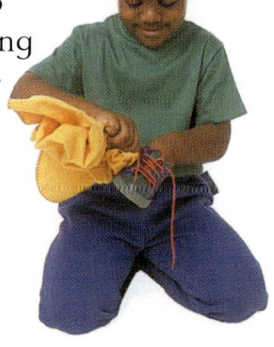

pond
A **pond** is a small lake.

a b c d e f g h i j k l m n o **p** q r s t u v w x y z

pony
A **pony** is a small horse.

potato
A **potato** is a vegetable that grows in the ground.

pour
To **pour** a liquid is to tip it out of a container.

present
A **present** is a parcel that you give to someone on a special occasion.

poppy
A **poppy** is a flower with big red, orange, yellow, or white petals.

price
The **price** of something is the amount of money you have to pay for it.

porcupine
A **porcupine** is an animal with pointed hairs called quills.

prickle
A **prickle** is a sharp point, like the ones on this chestnut.

prawn
A **prawn** is a sea animal with a hard shell and long antennae.

prince
A **prince** is the son of a king and queen. A **princess** is the daughter of a king and queen.

post office
A **post office** is a place where you can buy stamps, and post letters and parcels. A **postal worker** is someone who works in a post office.

A B C D E F G H I J K L M N O P Q R S T U V W X Y Z

prize
A **prize** is a reward you may be given if you win a competition.

pump
A **pump** is a machine that pushes liquid or air into something. This pump pushes air into a bicycle tyre.

puppy
A **puppy** is a young dog.

propeller
A **propeller** is the blades that spin round to power aeroplanes or boats.

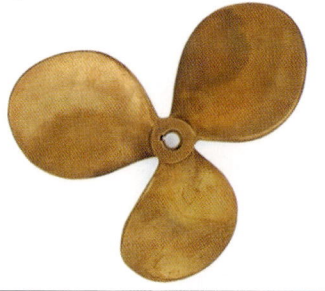

puncture
A **puncture** is a small hole, in a tyre, that lets the air out.

purple
Purple is a colour. It is made by mixing blue and red.

puddle
A **puddle** is a pool of muddy water.

pupa
A **pupa** is a caterpillar changing into a butterfly or a moth.

push
To **push** is to take hold of something and move it away from you. 

pull
To **pull** is to take hold of something and move it towards you.

puppet
A **puppet** is a doll that is moved by strings or your fingers.

a b c d e f g h i j k l m n o p q r s t u v w x y z

puzzle
A **puzzle** is a game or a problem that you enjoy trying to work out.

pyramid
A **pyramid** is a building with a square base and sloping, triangular sides. Ancient peoples built pyramids.

python
A **python** is a large snake that kills its prey by squeezing it to death.

Q

Qq Qq Qq Qq

quarry
A **quarry** is a place where stone is cut out of the ground. The stone is used for building.

quarter
A **quarter** is one of four equal parts. Four quarters make a whole.

queen
A **queen** is a woman who heads a country. Queens live in palaces.

quick
To be **quick** is to do something in a short time.

quiet
To be **quiet** is to make no noise at all.

quilt
A **quilt** is a warm, soft covering for a bed.

quiz
A **quiz** is a game in which people try to answer lots of questions.

A B C D E F G H I J K L M N O P Q R S T U V W X Y Z

R

Rr *Rr* Rr *Rr*

rabbit
A **rabbit** is a small, furry animal with long ears.

race
A **race** is a competition to find out who is the fastest.

racing car
A **racing car** is a type of car that goes very fast around a track.

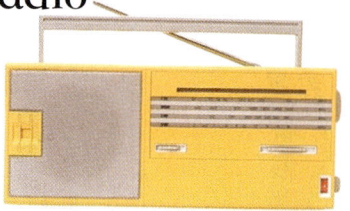

radio
A **radio** is a machine that receives sound waves from the air. It turns them into music or voices that you can listen to.

raft
A **raft** is a flat boat that is made out of logs.

railway
A **railway** is a track for trains to run along. The track is made from long strips of metal called **rails**.

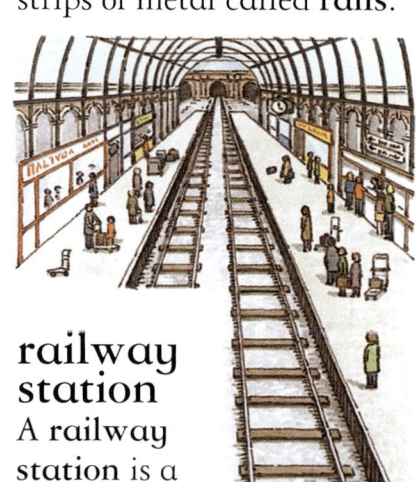

railway station
A **railway station** is a place where you go to buy a ticket and catch a train.

rain
Rain is drops of water that fall from clouds in the sky.

rainbow
A **rainbow** is an arc of different colours that appears in the sky when the sun shines through rain. The seven colours of the rainbow are: red, orange, yellow, green, blue, **indigo**, and **violet**.

reach
To **reach** for something is to stretch out your hand to take or touch it. This boy is reaching for his toys.

a b c d e f g h i j k l m n o p q **r** s t u v w x y z

read

To **read** is to understand the meaning of written or printed words.

record

A **record** is a circle of flat plastic that stores sounds like music. You use a **record player** to listen to a record.

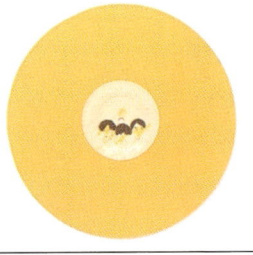

recorder

A **recorder** is a wooden or plastic musical instrument. You play a recorder by blowing down it and covering the holes with your fingers.

rectangle

A **rectangle** is a shape with two long sides, two shorter sides, and four corners.

red

Red is a colour. Tomatoes are red.

refrigerator

A **refrigerator** is a metal cupboard. It has a machine inside for keeping food cold.

repair

To **repair** something is to mend it.

reptile

A **reptile** is a cold-blooded animal with a backbone. Most reptiles are covered with scales. Snakes and lizards are reptiles.

lizard

snake

rescue

To **rescue** someone or something is to save them from danger or harm.

restaurant

A **restaurant** is a place where you can buy and eat a meal.

rhinoceros

A **rhinoceros** is a large, heavy animal with a thick skin. It has one or two horns on the top of its nose.

ribbon

A **ribbon** is a thin strip of material that you use to tie up gifts or hair.

A B C D E F G H I J K L M N O P Q **R** S T U V W X Y Z

rice
Rice is the small, white seeds of a plant that grows in wet ground in hot countries.

ride
To **ride** is to sit in or on something as it moves along. This girl is riding a horse.

right
Right is the opposite of left. This girl is making a right turn on her bicycle.

ring
A **ring** is a circle of metal that you wear on your finger. 

ring
When something **rings**, it makes the sound of a bell.

river
A **river** is a large stream of water that flows into another river, a lake, or the sea.

road
A **road** is a hard, smooth track for cars, lorries, and other traffic to drive on. There are many different types of roads.

robot
A **robot** is a machine that can move and do some jobs that people can do.

rock
A **rock** is a large, heavy stone found in the ground. 

rocket
A **rocket** is a metal tube full of gases. The gases make the power to send spacecraft into space.

roll
To **roll** is to turn over and over as you move along.

a b c d e f g h i j k l m n o p q **r** s t u v w x y z

roof
A **roof** is the part that covers the top of a building.

room
A **room** is part of a building. A room has a **ceiling**, a **floor**, four **walls**, and a door.

root
A **root** is the part of a plant that grows underground. Roots take up water from the soil to feed the plant.

root

rope
Rope is strong, thick string. Ropes are used to pull or lift heavy things. 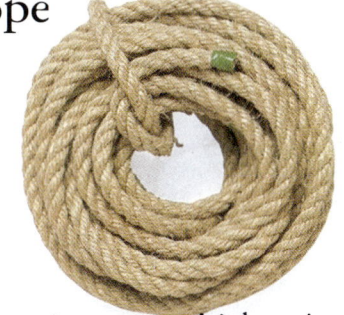

rose
A **rose** is a sweet-smelling flower with lots of petals, and thorns on its stem.

round
When something is **round**, it is shaped like a circle or a ball.

row
A **row** is a straight line of things.

rug
A **rug** is a piece of material that covers part of a floor.

ruler
A **ruler** is a piece of wood that you use to draw and measure straight lines.

run
To **run** is to move very quickly on two legs.

runway
A **runway** is a strip of flat, smooth ground where aircraft can take off and land.

A B C D E F G H I J K L M N O P Q R **S** T U V W X Y Z

S

Ss Ss Ss Ss

sad
A **sad** person is someone who feels unhappy.

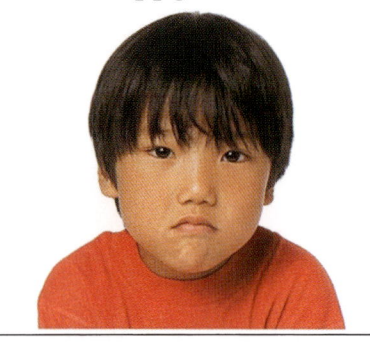

saddle
A **saddle** is the seat you sit on when you ride on a horse.

sail
A **sail** is a large piece of material attached to a boat. Wind blows into the sails to move the boat through the water.

sail
To **sail** is to travel on a boat. A **sailor** is a person who works on a boat. A **sailing boat** is a boat that is moved along by wind in its sails.

salad
A **salad** is a cold mixture of vegetables like lettuce, radishes, and mushrooms.

salt
Salt is a white powder made from minerals found in sea water. Salt is used to flavour food.

same
When two things are the **same**, they are like each other in every way.

sand
Sand is grains of rock that cover a beach or desert.

sand-castle

sandwich
A **sandwich** is two pieces of bread with a tasty filling between them.

satellite
A **satellite** is any object that moves around a planet in space. Man-made satellites move around the Earth collecting information.

satellite dish
A **satellite dish** is a machine that receives information from a satellite.

a b c d e f g h i j k l m n o p q r s t u v w x y z

saucepan
A **saucepan** is a metal container you use for cooking.

saw
A **saw** is a tool that has a blade with sharp, metal teeth. You use a saw to cut wood.

scale
A **scale** is a hard, thin piece of skin on a fish or a reptile. This fish is covered with hundreds of scales.

scales
Scales are a machine that is used to weigh things.

scarf
A **scarf** is a long piece of material worn around your neck.

school
A **school** is a place where you go to learn. At school your teacher teaches you important things such as how to read, write, and count.

scientist
A **scientist** is a person who studies a science like chemistry.

scissors
Scissors are a tool with two sharp blades. You use scissors to cut things.

scorpion
A **scorpion** is an animal with two large claws and a poisonous sting in its tail.

scratch
To **scratch** yourself is to rub your skin with your fingernails to stop it from itching.

screw
A **screw** is a kind of nail with grooves.

scrub
To **scrub** is to rub something with a wet brush. This girl is scrubbing her nails.

69

A B C D E F G H I J K L M N O P Q R **S** T U V W X Y Z

sea
The **sea** is the part of the Earth that is salt water. Fish live in the sea.

seagull
A **seagull** is a sea bird with grey and white feathers.

seahorse
A **seahorse** is a fish with a head like a horse's head and a long tail.

seal
A **seal** is a large sea animal with grey fur and whiskers. Seals have flippers that help them to swim.

season

spring   summer

autumn   winter

A **season** is a time of year. There are four seasons and they always follow the same order: **spring**, **summer**, **autumn**, and **winter**.

seat-belt
A **seat-belt** is a safety strap in a vehicle. You wear a seat-belt around your body in case there is an accident.

seaweed
Seaweed is a plant that grows in the sea.

seed
A **seed** is the part of a plant that grows into a new plant.

seesaw
A **seesaw** is a balancing toy for two people. They sit at opposite ends of a long plank and rock up and down.

sell
To **sell** something is to give it to someone in return for money.

seven
Seven is the number that comes after six and before eight.

sew
To **sew** is to join material together using a needle and thread.

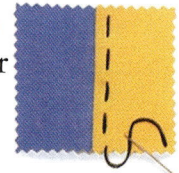

70

a b c d e f g h i j k l m n o p q r **s** t u v w x y z

shadow
A **shadow** is a dark shape that you make when you stand in the way of light.

shark
A **shark** is a large sea animal with lots of big, sharp teeth. 

shelf
A **shelf** is a long piece of wood that you keep things on.

shell
sea shell 

A **shell** is the hard, outside covering of an egg, a nut, or an animal.

shake
To **shake** something is to move it quickly up and down and from side to side.

sharp
When something is **sharp**, it has an edge or a point that can cut things.

ship
A **ship** is a large boat that sails on the sea. Passenger ships carry people. 

shape
A **shape** is the pattern you make when you draw round something. Circles, squares, triangles, and rectangles are all shapes.

sheep
A **sheep** is a farm animal with a thick, woolly coat. A female sheep is called a **ewe** and a male sheep is a **ram**.

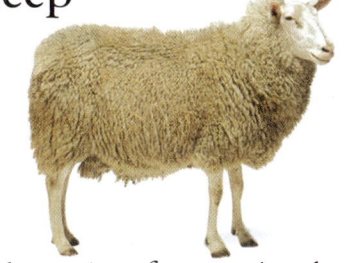

shirt
A **shirt** is a garment that you wear on the top part of your body.

share
To **share** is to divide something into pieces and give some of it away. This boy is sharing his lunch with a friend.

shoe
A **shoe** is a strong covering for your foot. Shoes protect your feet from the hard ground.

A B C D E F G H I J K L M N O P Q R **S** T U V W X Y Z

shop
A **shop** is a building where you can buy things.

short
When something is **short**, it is not long.

shoulder
Your **shoulder** is the part of your body between your neck and arm.

shout
To **shout** is to speak very loudly.

shower
A **shower** is a spray of water that you stand under to wash yourself.

shut
When something is **shut**, it is not open.

sing
To **sing** is to make music with your voice.

sink
When something **sinks**, it is too heavy to float and so it drops beneath the water.

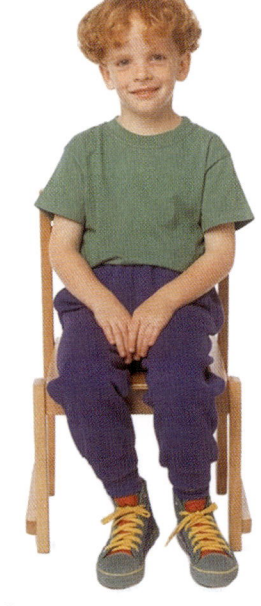

sit
To **sit** is to rest your bottom on a chair or on the floor.

six
Six is the number that comes after five and before seven.

skate
To **skate** is to glide over ice wearing special boots with metal blades called **ice skates**.

a b c d e f g h i j k l m n o p q r **s** t u v w x y z

skeleton
A **skeleton** is an animal's bones all joined together. You have a skeleton inside your body.

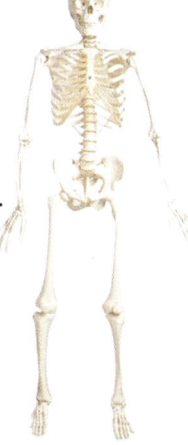

ski
To **ski** is to slide down snowy mountains wearing **skis** on your feet.

skis

skip
To **skip** is to jump over a **skipping rope** as it turns. You can also skip without a rope. 

skirt
A **skirt** is a garment that hangs down from the waist.

sky
The **sky** is the space above your head where you can see the sun and clouds.

skyscraper
A **skyscraper** is a very tall building that looks as if it is touching the sky.

sledge
A **sledge** is a vehicle made out of wood with smooth, metal runners on the bottom. A sledge is used to carry people over snow.

sleep
To **sleep** is to close your eyes and rest your body and mind. You go to sleep at night, or when you are tired.

slice
A **slice** is a thin piece of something.

slide
A **slide** is a kind of toy. You climb to the top of the ladder and drop down a slippery slope.

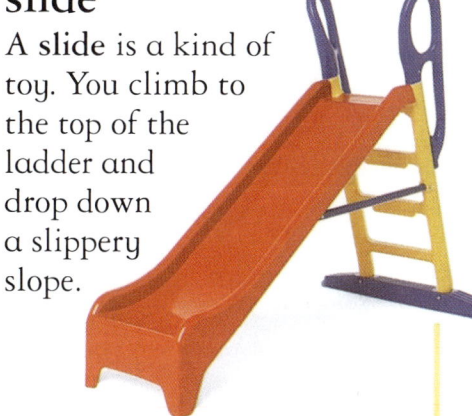

slow
When something is **slow**, it takes a long time. This tortoise is very slow to move from one place to another. 

small
When something is **small**, it is little and not very big.

73

smile
When you **smile**, your face shows that you are happy.

snail
A **snail** is an animal with a soft body and a shell on its back.

snake
A **snake** is an animal with a long, thin body, a scaly skin, and no legs.

snow
Snow is tiny, white flakes of frozen water. Snow falls from clouds in cold weather.

snowman
A **snowman** is a model of a person made out of snow.

soap
Soap is a material that you use with water to wash away dirt.

soccer
Soccer is a ball game played by two teams of eleven players who kick a ball to score goals.

sock
A **sock** is a soft covering for your foot. You wear socks inside shoes.

sofa
A **sofa** is a long, cushioned seat with a back and arms. Two or three people can sit on a sofa.

soldier
A **soldier** is a person who is a member of an army.

solid
When something is **solid**, it keeps its shape and is firm and hard.

space
Space is the place above the Earth where there is no air. The planets are in space.

spacecraft
A **spacecraft** is a vehicle that travels in space.

spade
A **spade** is a tool that you use for digging. It has a long handle and a wide, flat blade.

a b c d e f g h i j k l m n o p q r **s** t u v w x y z

sparrow
A **sparrow** is a small, brown bird. Sparrows are often seen in gardens.

sport
A **sport** is a game or a competition to exercise your body. There are lots of different sports like running and high jumping.

spider
A **spider** is an animal with eight hairy legs. Spiders spin webs to catch small insects to eat.

square
A **square** is a shape with four corners and four equal sides.

squash
To **squash** something is to press it and make it flat.

squirrel
A **squirrel** is a furry animal with a long, bushy tail. Squirrels live in trees and eat nuts.

stable
A **stable** is a building for a horse to live in.

spill
To **spill** something is to accidentally knock it out of its container.

squeeze
To **squeeze** something is to press it. This girl is squeezing an orange.

spoon
A **spoon** is a tool that you use to pick up food.

stamp
A **stamp** is a small piece of sticky paper that you put on an envelope. A stamp shows that you have paid to post a letter.

A B C D E F G H I J K L M N O P Q R **S** T U V W X Y Z

stand
To **stand** is to be on your feet without moving.

star
A **star** is one of the bright lights that shine in the sky at night.

starfish
A **starfish** is a sea animal with five arms that make the shape of a star.

start
To **start** is to begin something. This boy is starting a race.

steering wheel
A **steering wheel** is the part of a car that you hold to turn the wheels.

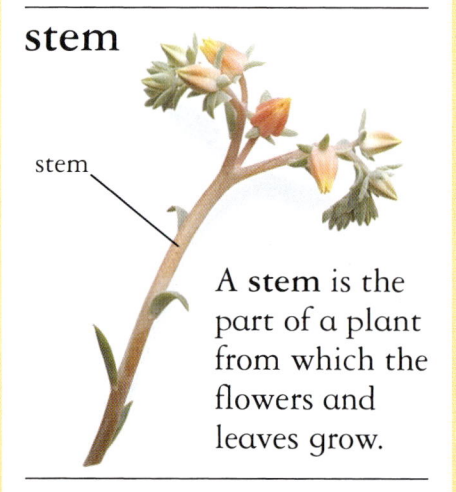

stem
A **stem** is the part of a plant from which the flowers and leaves grow.

stone
A **stone** is a small, hard piece of rock.

stopwatch
A **stopwatch** is a special kind of watch that you use to time a race.

strawberry
A **strawberry** is a small, red, juicy fruit.

stream
A **stream** is a small river.

string
String is a strong, thick thread that you use to tie things together.

stripe
A **stripe** is a narrow band of colour. This girl is wearing a striped T-shirt.

a b c d e f g h i j k l m n o p q r **s** t u v w x y z

submarine
A **submarine** is a type of ship that travels underwater.

sugar
Sugar is a food sometimes made from sugar-cane. You use sugar to sweeten other foods.

sun
The **sun** is the huge, burning star that gives the Earth heat and light.

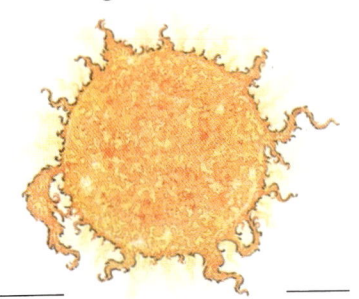

sunglasses
Sunglasses are dark glasses that you wear to protect your eyes from strong sunlight.

supermarket
A **supermarket** is a large shop that sells food and things for the house.

swan
A **swan** is a large water bird with a long neck and webbed feet.

swim
To **swim** is to move yourself through water using your arms and legs.

swimming pool
A **swimming pool** is a place where you swim.

swing
A **swing** is a hanging seat that you sit on and move backwards and forwards.

sword
A **sword** is a long, metal blade with a handle at one end.

synagogue
A **synagogue** is a building where Jewish people meet to pray.

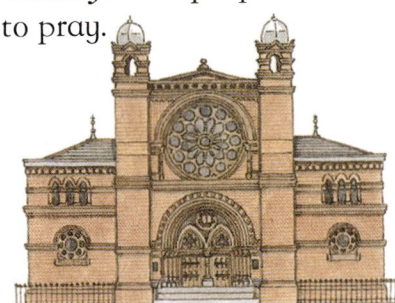

77

A B C D E F G H I J K L M N O P Q R S **T** U V W X Y Z

T
Tt *Tt* Tt Tt

table
A **table** is a piece of furniture with a flat top and legs.

tadpole
A **tadpole** is a tiny animal that lives in a pond. Tadpoles grow into frogs.

tail
A **tail** is the part of an animal's body that sticks out at the back.

tall
When something is **tall**, it is higher than usual. The girl in the red T-shirt is taller than her friend.

tambourine
A **tambourine** is a round musical instrument with metal rings. You shake a tambourine to make a sound.

taxi
A **taxi** is a car that you travel in and then pay the driver.

tea
Tea is a drink made from the dried leaves of a tea-plant.

teacher
A **teacher** is a person who helps you to learn things.

team
A **team** is a group of people who work or play together.

tear
A **tear** is a drop of water that comes out of your eye.

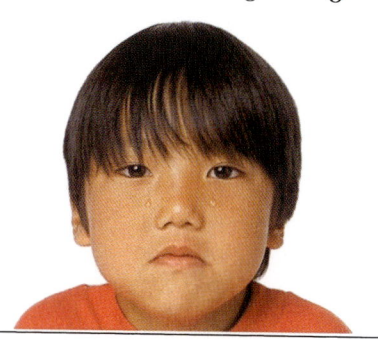

tear
To **tear** something is to pull it apart.

telephone
A **telephone** is an instrument for talking to someone who is far away.

78

a b c d e f g h i j k l m n o p q r s **t** u v w x y z

telescope
A **telescope** is an instrument that makes faraway objects look bigger and closer.

television
A **television** is a machine that receives messages sent through the air and turns them into sounds and pictures.

temple
A **temple** is a building where people go to pray.

ten
Ten is the number that comes after nine and before eleven.

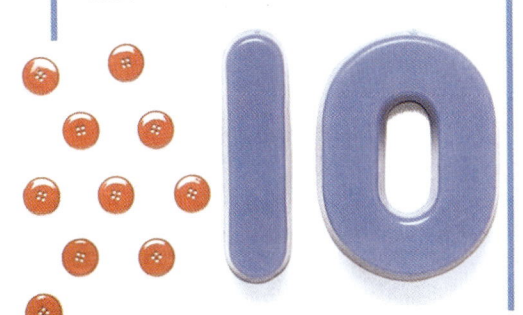

tennis
Tennis is a game in which two or four players hit a ball, with a racket, over a net.

tent
A **tent** is a cloth shelter for camping in.

theatre
A **theatre** is a building where you go to see plays being acted on a stage.

thermometer
A **thermometer** is an instrument that measures how hot or cold something is. You can take your **temperature** with a thermometer.

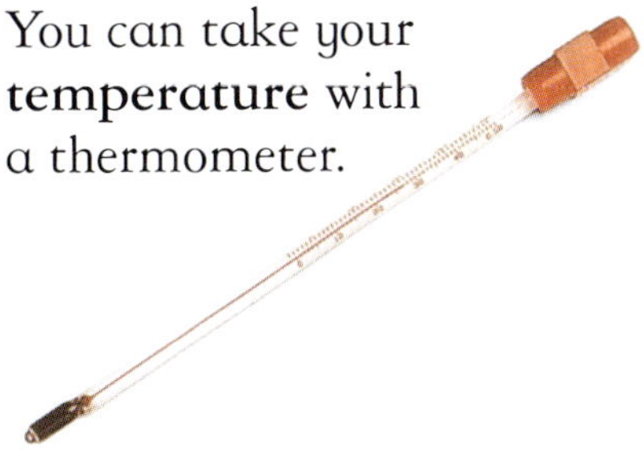

thigh
Your **thigh** is the part of your leg between your hip and your knee. 

thin
When something is **thin**, it is not fat or thick.

thistle
A **thistle** is a prickly plant with a purple flower.

thorn
A **thorn** is a sharp point on the stem of some plants.

thorn

thread
A **thread** is a thin strand of cotton.

A B C D E F G H I J K L M N O P Q R S T U V W X Y Z

three
Three is the number that comes after two and before four.

tiger
A **tiger** is a wild, big cat with an orange and black striped coat. 

thumb
Your **thumb** is the thick, short finger nearest to your wrist.

tile
A **tile** is a thin, flat covering for walls and floors.

tired
When you feel **tired**, you need to rest or sleep.

ticket
A **ticket** is a piece of paper that shows you have paid to travel on a bus or get into places like the theatre. 

time
Time is a measurement in **hours**, **minutes**, and **seconds**.

toad
A **toad** is an animal that looks like a big frog with a rough, dry skin.

tie
A **tie** is a narrow strip of material that is tied around a shirt collar.

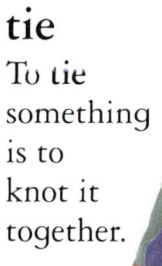

tiptoe
To **tiptoe** is to walk on your toes as quietly as you can.

tie
To **tie** something is to knot it together.

toboggan
A **toboggan** is like a small, flat sledge. You can slide down snowy slopes on a toboggan.

a b c d e f g h i j k l m n o p q r s t u v w x y z

toe
Your **toe** is one of the five parts on the end of your foot.

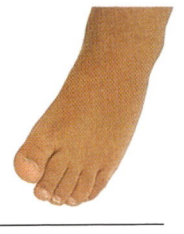

toilet
A **toilet** is where you go to get rid of the waste in your body.

tomato
A **tomato** is a round, red fruit that you eat in salads.

tongue
Your **tongue** is the long, soft part inside your mouth. You can lick things with your tongue.

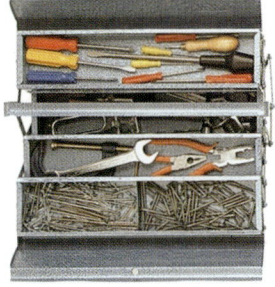

tool
A **tool** is an instrument that helps you to do a job. Spanners, screwdrivers, and pliers are all tools.

tooth
Your **tooth** is one of the white, bony parts in your mouth. You bite and chew with your **teeth**.

toothbrush
A **toothbrush** is a small brush that you use to clean your teeth. You put **toothpaste** on a toothbrush.

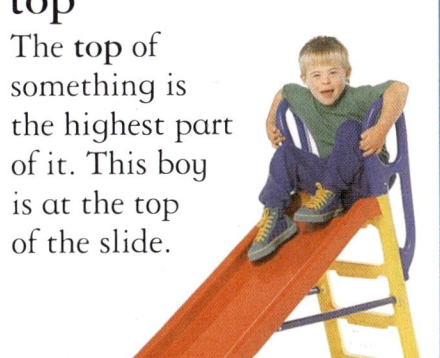

top
The **top** of something is the highest part of it. This boy is at the top of the slide.

tornado
A **tornado** is a very strong wind that whirls round and round. Tornados can rip up trees and knock down houses.

toucan
A **toucan** is a black and white bird with a large, brightly coloured beak.

tourist
A **tourist** is a person who visits places of interest.

81

A B C D E F G H I J K L M N O P Q R S **T** U V W X Y Z

towel
A **towel** is a piece of cloth you use to dry yourself with.

town
A **town** is a place with lots of houses, shops, and schools where people live and work.

toy
A **toy** is a plaything for you to have fun with.

tractor
A **tractor** is a farm machine that is used to pull heavy loads.

traffic
Traffic is all the cars, buses, motorbikes, and other vehicles that travel on the road.

train
A **train** is a line of railway carriages that are pulled along a track by an engine. Trains carry passengers from one place to another.

transparent
When something is **transparent**, it is clear so that you can see through it. This glass jug is transparent.

trapeze
A **trapeze** is a type of swing that is used by acrobats.

tray
A **tray** is a flat piece of wood or plastic that you use to carry food and drink.

treasure
Treasure is gold, silver, coins, jewels, and other precious things. A treasure-chest is a box where you keep valuable objects.

a b c d e f g h i j k l m n o p q r s t u v w x y z

tree
A **tree** is a large plant with leaves, branches, and a thick trunk.

triangle
A **triangle** is a shape with three straight sides and three corners.

trick
A **trick** is an amazing thing you can do to surprise people. This boy is pulling a lot of flowers out of a small box.

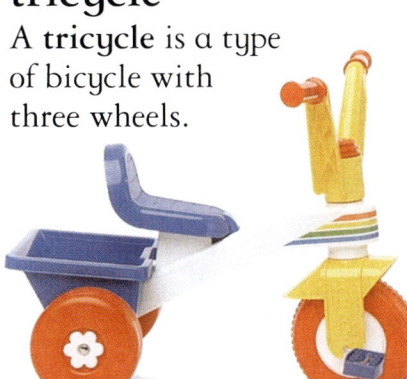

tricycle
A **tricycle** is a type of bicycle with three wheels.

trophy
A **trophy** is a large, metal cup that may be given as a prize.

trousers
Trousers are a piece of clothing that you wear on your legs.

truck
A **truck** is a big, powerful vehicle that is used to carry heavy loads. This truck has an open back for tipping out its load.

trumpet
valve

A **trumpet** is a musical instrument that is made out of brass. You blow into the mouthpiece and press the valves to make a sound.

trunk
A **trunk** is an elephant's long nose. Elephants use their trunks to squirt water into their mouths, and also to pick up things.

tugboat
A **tugboat** is a small, very powerful boat that is used to pull bigger boats in and out of harbour.

tulip
A **tulip** is a cup-shaped flower that grows from a bulb and blooms in the spring.

tunnel
A **tunnel** is a long passage cut through a hill or under the ground.

83

A B C D E F G H I J K L M N O P Q R S **T** **U** V W X Y Z

turkey
A **turkey** is a large, farm bird with black and white feathers and a long, red chin.

twig
A **twig** is a small, thin branch of a tree. Leaves grow on twigs.

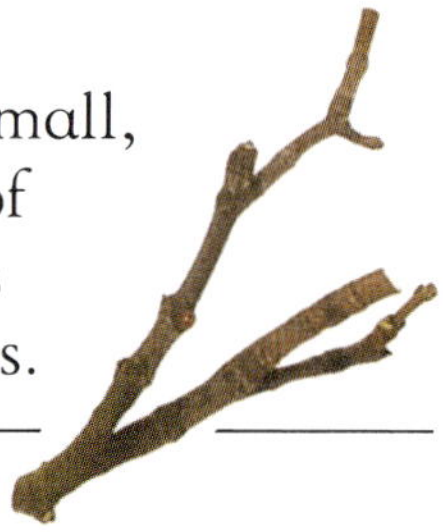

twin
A **twin** is one of two children that were born at the same time to the same parents.

U

Uu *Uu* Uu *Uu*

umbrella
An **umbrella** is a piece of waterproof material on a frame. An umbrella keeps you dry when it rains.

turtle
A **turtle** is a sea animal with a scaly body covered by a hard shell. Turtles live on land and in water.

two
Two is the number that comes after one and before three.

under
To be **under** something is to be below it. The toy soldier is standing under the arch.

tusk
A **tusk** is the long, pointed tooth of an elephant.

typewriter

A **typewriter** is a machine with keys that you press to print letters and numbers onto paper.

underwear
Underwear is clothing that you wear next to your skin, under your other clothes.

tusk

a b c d e f g h i j k l m n o p q r s t u v w x y z

V

Vv *Vv* Vv Vv

undress
To **undress** is to take off your clothes. You undress to get ready for bed.

unicorn
A **unicorn** is an imaginary animal. It looks like a horse with a long, twisted horn on its forehead.

university
A **university** is a place where you can go to learn after leaving school.

up
When something goes **up**, it moves to a higher place. This girl is throwing the ball up into the air.

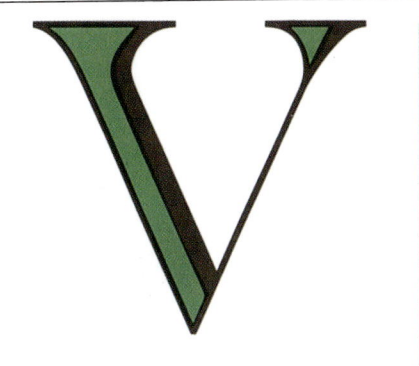

vacuum cleaner
A **vacuum cleaner** is a machine that sucks up dirt from the floor.

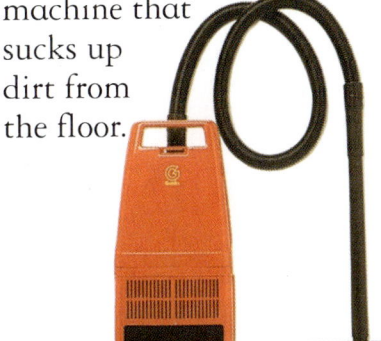

valley
A **valley** is the low land between two hills.

vase
A **vase** is a container for holding cut flowers.

vegetable
A **vegetable** is a plant with roots or leaves that you can eat either cooked or raw. There are lots of different kinds of vegetables.

vehicle
A **vehicle** is a machine that carries people and things from one place to another. Cars and trucks are vehicles.

vet
A **vet** is a type of doctor who cares for animals when they are sick or injured.

A B C D E F G H I J K L M N O P Q R S T U V **W** X Y Z

videotape
A **videotape** is a recording of pictures and sounds. You use a **videotape recorder** and a television to watch a videotape.

violin
A **violin** is a musical instrument made out of wood. You hold it under your chin and draw a bow across its strings.

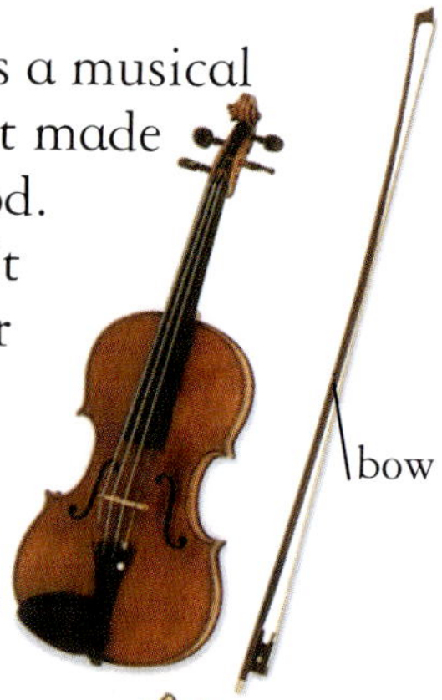

bow

W
WwWwWwWw

village
A **village** is a small group of houses and shops in the countryside.

volcano
A **volcano** is a mountain with a hole in the top. Sometimes hot melted rocks, gas, and ash burst out of a volcano. 

wagon
A **wagon** is a cart that is used to carry heavy loads. Wagons are sometimes pulled by horses.

waiter
A **waiter** is a person who serves food and drink in a restaurant.

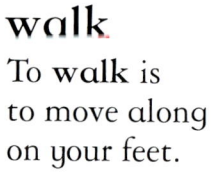

vine
A **vine** is a climbing plant. Grapes grow on vines in fields called **vineyards**.

vulture
A **vulture** is a large bird with a bald head. Vultures eat dead animals.

walk
To **walk** is to move along on your feet.

a b c d e f g h i j k l m n o p q r s t u v **w** x y z

walking stick
A **walking stick** is a long, thin piece of wood that you use to help you to walk.

wallaby
A **wallaby** is a small, furry animal that jumps like a kangaroo.

wallet
A **wallet** is a small, flat case that you keep your money in.

walrus
A **walrus** is a big sea animal with a large body and two long, curved tusks.

wash
To **wash** is to clean yourself with soap and water.

watch
To **watch** something is to look at it carefully.

watch
A **watch** is a small clock that you wear on your wrist.

water
Water is the clear liquid that comes out of a tap. Water falls from the sky as rain.

waterfall
A **waterfall** is a stream or river flowing over the edge of a rock.

waterlily
A **waterlily** is a flower that grows in ponds and lakes.

watermelon
A **watermelon** is a large fruit with a red, watery inside.

wave
To **wave** is to move your hand and signal hello or goodbye.

87

A B C D E F G H I J K L M N O P Q R S T U V **W** X Y Z

wear
To **wear** something is to put it on. This boy is wearing a hat on his head and clothes on his body.

wedding
A **wedding** is a special time when two people get married.

week
A **week** is a measurement of time that is seven days long. There are fifty-two weeks in one year.

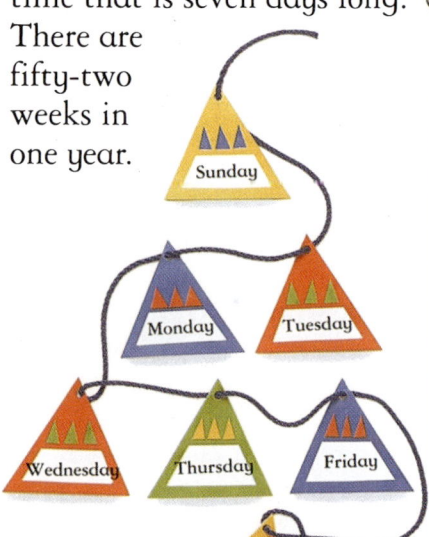

weigh
To **weigh** something is to find out how heavy it is.

wet
When something is **wet**, it is covered with water and is not dry. This dog is very wet and is shaking himself dry.

whale
A **whale** is a huge sea animal that breathes air. Whales are the largest living animals.

wheat
Wheat is a plant that is grown on a farm. We grind wheat to make flour.

wheel
A **wheel** is a round frame that turns on a rod in order to move things.

wheelbarrow
A **wheelbarrow** is a small cart with a wheel at the front. It can be used to move things like soil and stones.

wheelchair
A **wheelchair** is a special chair that you move about in if you have difficulty walking.

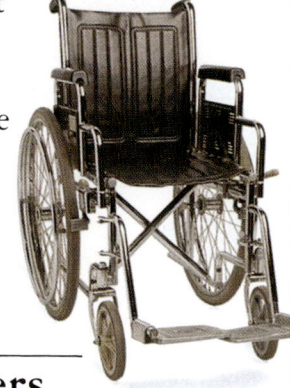

whiskers
Whiskers are the long hairs that grow on an animal's face.

a b c d e f g h i j k l m n o p q r s t u v **w** x y z

whisper
To **whisper** is to talk very quietly so that only one person can hear you.

whistle
A **whistle** is an instrument that makes a sharp, high sound when you blow it.

white
White is a colour. Snow and salt are white.

wide
When something is **wide**, it measures a lot from one side to the other.

wind
The **wind** is air that is moving quickly.

windmill
A **windmill** is a machine that uses the power of the wind to turn its sails. Wheat is ground into flour in a windmill.

window
A **window** is an opening in a wall that is filled with a pane of glass. Windows let in light and air.

wing
wing

Wings are the part of an animal that help it to fly.

wire
Wire is a thin, metal thread that is often covered with plastic.

witch
A **witch** is an imaginary woman with magical powers.

A **wizard** is an imaginary man with magical powers.

wolf
A **wolf** is a wild animal that looks like a large, fierce dog.

A B C D E F G H I J K L M N O P Q R S T U V **W** **X** Y Z

woman
A **woman** is a grown-up girl.

wood
Wood is the hard part of a tree that is used to make tables and chairs.

wool
Wool is the soft, curly hair of a sheep. Wool is spun into yarn and used for knitting or making cloth.

world
The **world** is the Earth and everything that lives on it.

worm
A **worm** is a long animal that lives in the ground.

wrinkle
A **wrinkle** is a crease in the skin. This dog has wrinkles.

wrist
Your **wrist** is the joint between your hand and your arm.

write
To **write** is to put words on paper so that people can read them.

X

Xx *Xx* Xx Xx

X-ray
An **X-ray** is a special photograph of the inside of your body. Doctors can look at an X-ray to find out if you are sick or injured.

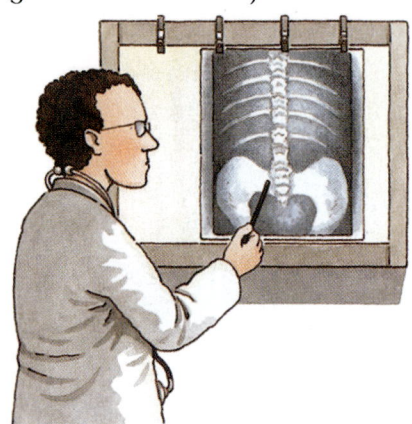

xylophone
A **xylophone** is a musical instrument that is made of metal or wooden bars. You hit the bars with beaters to make musical sounds.

a b c d e f g h i j k l m n o p q r s t u v w x y z

Y

Yy *Yy* Yy Yy

yacht
A **yacht** is a fast sailing boat with a cabin.

yawn
To **yawn** is to open your mouth wide and breathe in deeply. You yawn when you are tired.

year
A **year** is a measure of time that lasts 12 months, 52 weeks, or 365 days.

yellow
Yellow is a colour. Lemons are yellow.

yoghurt
Yoghurt is a thick, creamy food made from milk. Yoghurt often has fruit in it.

yolk
A **yolk** is the yellow part of an egg.

young
A **young** person is someone who is only a few years old. This baby is young.

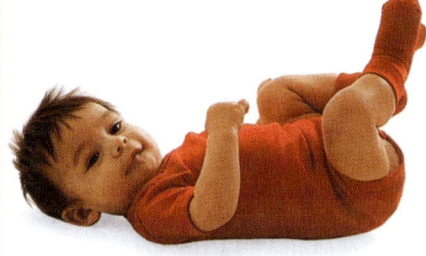

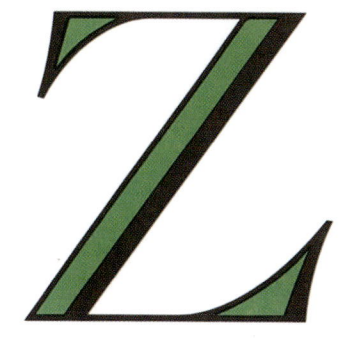

Z

Zz *Zz* Zz Zz

zebra
A **zebra** is an animal that looks like a horse with black and white stripes on its body.

zero
Zero is the number that comes before one. Zero means nothing.

zip
A **zip** is a fastener for clothes.

zoo
A **zoo** is a place where wild animals are kept for people to visit and learn about.

A B C D E F G H I J K L M N O P Q R S T U V W X Y Z

Wörterbuchspiele

Versuche, alle diese Worträtsel mit Hilfe des Wörterbuchs zu lösen. Dabei übst du, Wörter und ihre Schreibweise nachzusehen. Alle Antworten auf die Rätsel stehen irgendwo im Wörterbuch. Die Bilder helfen dir, die Wörter leichter zu finden.

Vor jedem Spiel steht ein Lösungsbeispiel, damit du siehst, wie es funktioniert. Schreibe die Antworten nicht in dieses Buch, sondern auf ein Blatt Papier. Das Meiste kannst du allein herausfinden, manchmal wirst du aber auch Freunde brauchen, die dir bei den Lösungen helfen. Viel Spaß.

Leichte Wörterbuchspiele haben einen *, mittlere zwei **, schwierigere drei *** Sterne.

Tieralphabet *

Diese Tiere sollten in alphabetischer Reihenfolge stehen, aber hier sind sie alle durcheinander. Benütze das Alphabet auf der Seite ganz oben zum Sortieren.

armadillo

elephant

rabbit

dinosaur

tiger

pelican

vulture

Worträtsel **

Kennst du schon englische Wörter, die zu diesen Bildern passen? Die Anfangsbuchstaben helfen dir, im Wörterbuch nach den Namen zu suchen. Lass dir eine lustige Geschichte mit diesen Wörtern erzählen.

acrobat

c

p

y

e

s

w

d

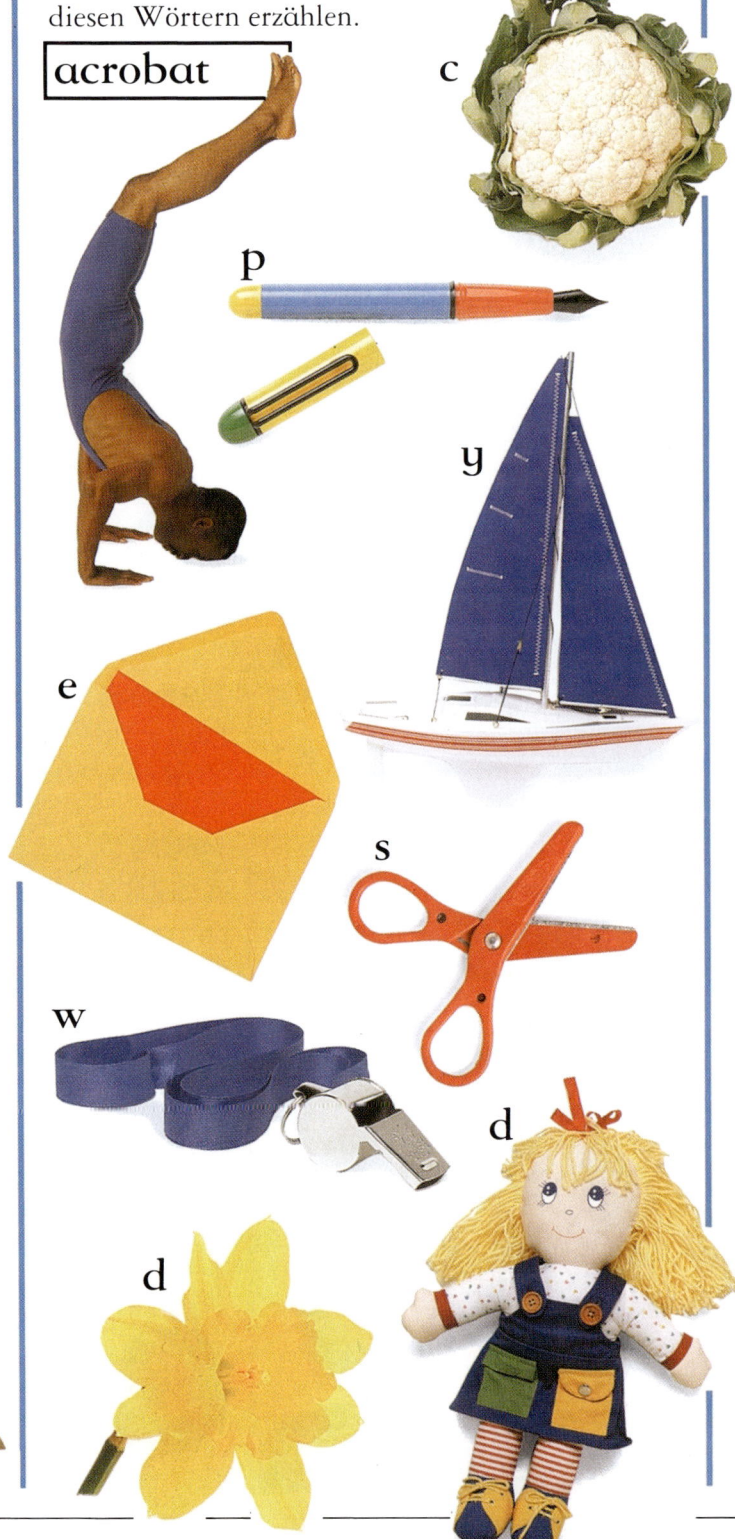

d

a b c d e f g h i j k l m n o p q r s t u v w x y z

Wortdetektiv ***

Beantworte die Fragen mit dem richtigen Wort. Nutze die Hinweise, indem du dein Rätsel wie ein Detektiv Schritt für Schritt löst.

> • What do you call a person who breaks into a building to steal something?
> The word begins with the letter **b**.
> **burglar**

• What is the name for precious things like gold, silver, coins, and jewels?
Look for the things that sparkle on page 82.

• What can you wear over your face to disguise yourself?
Find the hidden face under **m**.

• What do you call a person who keeps law and order?
Look for a word beginning with **p**.

• What does a detective use to find the clues left behind by a burglar?
Try page 47.

Wörterbuchzielen *

Dieses Spiel kannst du allein oder mit einem Freund oder einer Freundin spielen.

1) Denk dir einen Buchstaben aus dem Alphabet aus.
2) Schließe das Wörterbuch und versuche, es genau bei dem Buchstaben zu öffnen, den du ausgewählt hast.

Wenn du genau triffst, bekommst du zwei Punkte, wenn du nahe dran bist, einen Punkt.

Prüfe dein Gedächtnis **

Einige Wörter, die zu den Bildern gehören, kennst du vielleicht schon. Die anderen suchst du dir aus dem Wörterbuch heraus. Schreibe alle Wörter auf ein Blatt Papier. Dann verdeckst du das Blatt und siehst dir die Bilder an. An wie viele englische Bezeichnungen der Dinge erinnerst du dich?

93

A B C D E F G H I J K L M N O P Q R S T U V W X Y Z

Falsches raus! **

Wenn du diese Bilder sorgfältig ansiehst, wirst du bemerken, dass in jeder Gruppe eines dabei ist, das nicht dazu passt. Kannst du es finden? Lass dir dazu die Beschreibung im Wörterbuch vorlesen.

snake **beetle** **bee**

This **snake** is the odd one out because it is not an insect.

crown **glove** **hat**

grape **pear** **carrot**

trumpet **recorder** **violin**

Finde das Wort ***

Benutze das Wortregister am Ende des Buches, um die folgenden Fragen zu beantworten. Schlag alle fett gedruckten Wörter dort nach. So wirst du die Seitenzahl finden, wo sie erklärt sind.

- What do you do in a **cinema**? You watch a film in a cinema.

- Who do **guide dogs** help?

- What is a **stallion**?

- How do **fire fighters** travel to a fire?

- Why do people send out **invitations**?

- Is there another word for a **rainforest**?

- **Mars** is a planet, can you name any others?

Sie klingen gleich **

Manche Wörter klingen gleich, haben aber verschiedene Bedeutungen. Sprich diese Wörter zusammen mit einem Freund laut aus, und dann schlagt abwechselnd nach, welche Bedeutung sie haben. Kennst du mehr solcher Wortpaare?

bat
A **bat** is a kind of stick that you use to hit a ball.

bat
A **bat** is a small, furry animal with wings.

cricket	cricket
flour	flower
nut	nut
orange	orange
pair	pear
right	write
tie	tie

a b c d e f g h i j k l m n o p q r s t u v w x y z

Tierwirrwarr *

Die Tiere auf dieser Seite sind alle durcheinander. Beantworte die Fragen, damit du herausfindest, welche Tiere zusammengehören. Sie können auch zu mehreren Gruppen gehören. Die Beschreibungen im Wörterbuch helfen dir.

toucan

Which of these birds cannot fly?

sheep

jaguar

dog

dolphin

crab

lamb

ostrich

How many of these birds can swim?

Can you match the mothers with their babies?

gosling

kitten

penguin

starfish

cat

Which of these animals live in, or around, water?

goose

There are three cats on this page. Can you point to them?

puppy

crocodile

95

A B C D E F G H I J K L M N O P Q R S T U V W X Y Z

Register

A (Seite 4–6)

above	[əˈbʌv]	über
accident	[ˈæksɪdənt]	Unfall
acrobat	[ˈækrəbæt]	Akrobat
to act	[ækt]	schauspielen
actor	[ˈæktə(r)]	Schauspieler
to add	[æd]	addieren, hinzufügen
adress	[əˈdres]	Adresse
adult	[ˈædʌlt]	Erwachsener
aeroplane	[ˈeərəpleɪn]	Flugzeug
africa	[ˈæfrɪkə]	Afrika
afternoon	[ˌa:ftəˈnu:n]	Nachmittag
airport	[ˈeəpɔ:t]	Flughafen
alligator	[ˈælɪgeɪtə(r)]	Alligator
alphabet	[ˈælfəbet]	Alphabet
ambulance	[ˈæmbjʊləns]	Krankenwagen
anchor	[ˈæŋkə(r)]	Anker
angry	[ˈæŋgrɪ]	verärgert
animal	[ˈænɪml]	Tier
ankle	[ˈæŋkl]	Knöchel
to answer	[ˈa:nsə(r)]	antworten
ant	[ænt]	Ameise
Antarctica	[ænˈta:ktɪkə]	Antarktis
ape	[eɪp]	Menschenaffe
apple	[ˈæpl]	Apfel
apple blossom	[ˈæplˈblɒsəm]	Apfelblüte
aquarium	[əˈkweərɪəm]	Aquarium
are	[a:r]	bist, seid, sind
arm	[ˈa:m]	Arm
armadillo	[ˌa:(r)məˈdɪloʊ]	Gürteltier
armour	[ˈa:mə(r)]	Rüstung
army	[ˈa:mɪ]	Armee
arrow	[ˈærəʊ]	Pfeil
artist	[ˈa:tɪst]	Künstler
Asia	[ˈeɪʃə]	Asien
to ask	[ɑ:sk]	fragen
astronaut	[ˈæstrənɔ:]	Astronaut
athlete	[ˈæθli:t]	Athlet
audience	[ˈɔ:dɪəns]	Publikum
aunt	[a:nt, ænt]	Tante
Australasia	[ˌɔ:strəˈleɪʒə]	Australasien
author	[ˈɔ:θə(r)]	Autor
autumn	[ˈɔ:təm]	Herbst
avalanche	[ˈævəlɑ:nʃ]	Lawine

B (Seite 6–13)

baby	[ˈbeɪbɪ]	Baby
back	[bæk]	Rücken, Rückseite
to bake	[beɪk]	backen
baker	[ˈbeɪkə(r)]	Bäcker
bakery	[ˈbeɪkərɪ]	Bäckerei
ball	[bɔ:l]	Ball
balloon	[bəˈlu:n]	Ballon
banana	[bəˈna:nə]	Banane
band	[bænd]	Band
bandage	[ˈbændɪdʒ]	Verband
bank	[bæŋk]	Flussufer
bank	[bæŋk]	Bank
barbecue	[ˈba:bɪkju:]	Grill
barley	[ˈbalɪ]	Gerste
barn	[ba:n]	Scheune
baseball	[ˈbeɪsbɔ:l]	Baseball
basket	[ˈba:skɪt]	Korb
bat	[bæt]	Schläger
bat	[bæt]	Fledermaus
bath	[ba:θ]	Badewanne
bathroom	[ba:θru:m]	Badezimmer
battery	[ˈbætərɪ]	Batterie
to be	[bi:]	sein
beach	[bi:tʃ]	Strand
beak	[bi:k]	Schnabel
bear	[beə(r)]	Bär
beard	[bɪəd]	Bart
bed	[bed]	Bett
bedroom	[ˈbedrʊm]	Schlafzimmer
bee	[bi:]	Biene
beetle	[ˈbi:tl]	Käfer
behind	[bɪˈhaɪnd]	hinter
bell	[bel]	Glocke
below	[bɪˈləʊ]	unter
belt	[belt]	Gürtel
bench	[bentʃ]	Bank
berry	[ˈberɪ]	Beere
between	[bɪˈtwi:n]	zwischen
bicycle	[ˈbaɪsɪkl]	Fahrrad
big	[bɪg]	groß
bike	[baɪk]	Fahrrad
billy goat	[ˈbɪlɪgəʊt]	Ziegenbock
bird	[bɜ:d]	Vogel
birthday	[ˈbɜ:θdeɪ]	Geburtstag
birthday cake	[ˈbɜ:θdeɪkeɪk]	Geburtstagstorte
birthday card	[ˈbɜ:θdeɪka:(r)d]	Geburtstagskarte
to bite	[baɪt]	beißen
black	[blæk]	schwarz
blanket	[ˈblæŋkɪt]	Decke
blind	[blaɪnd]	blind
blood	[blʌd]	Blut
blossom	[ˈblɒsəm]	Blüte
blouse	[blaʊz]	Bluse
to blow	[bləʊ]	blasen
blue	[blu:]	blau
boar	[bɔ:(r)]	Eber
boat	[bəʊt]	Boot
body	[ˈbɒdɪ]	Körper
bolt	[bəʊlt]	Schraube
bone	[bəʊn]	Knochen
book	[bʊk]	Buch
boomerang	[ˈbu:məræn]	Bumerang
bottle	[ˈbɒtl]	Flasche
bottom	[ˈbɒtəm]	Unterseite, Boden
bow	[bəʊ]	Bogen
bowl	[bəʊl]	Schüssel
box	[bɒks]	Schachtel
boy	[bɔɪ]	Junge
brain	[breɪn]	Gehirn
branch	[ˈbra:ntʃ]	Ast
bread	[bred]	Brot
to break	[breɪk]	brechen
breakfast	[ˈbrekfəst]	Frühstück
brick	[brɪk]	Ziegel
bride	[braɪd]	Braut
bridegroom	[ˈbraɪdgrʊm]	Bräutigam
bridge	[brɪdʒ]	Brücke
to bring	[brɪŋ]	bringen
brother	[ˈbrʌðə(r)]	Bruder
brown	[braʊn]	braun
brush	[brʌʃ]	Bürste
to brush	[brʌʃ]	bürsten
bucket	[ˈbʌkɪt]	Kübel
bud	[bʌd]	Knospe
to build	[bɪld]	bauen
builder	[ˈbɪlə(r)]	Baumeister
building	[ˈbɪldɪŋ]	Gebäude
bulb	[bʌlb]	Zwiebel, Knolle

A B C D E F G H I J K L M N O P Q R S T U V W X Y Z

bulb	[bʌlb]	Glühbirne
bull	[bʊl]	Stier
bulldozer	[ˈbʊldəʊzə(r)]	Bulldozer
burglar	[ˈbɜːglə(r)]	Einbrecher
bus	[bʌs]	Bus
bus driver	[bʌsˈdraɪvə(r)]	Busfahrer
bus-stop	[bʌsstɒp]	Bushaltestelle
butcher	[ˈbʊtʃə(r)]	Metzger
butter	[ˈbʌtə(r)]	Butter
butterfly	[ˈbʌtəflaɪ]	Schmetterling
button	[ˈbʌtn]	Knopf
to buy	[baɪ]	kaufen

C (Seite 13–21)

cabbage	[ˈkæbɪdʒ]	Kohl
cabin	[ˈkæbɪn]	Hütte
cactus	[ˈkæktəs]	Kaktus
calculator	[ˈkælkjʊleɪtə(r)]	Taschenrechner
calendar	[ˈkæləndə(r)]	Kalender
calf	[kaːf]	Kalb
camel	[ˈkæml]	Kamel
camera	[ˈkæmərə]	Kamera
to camp	[kæmp]	campen
campsite	[ˈkæmpsait]	Campingplatz
can	[kæn]	Konserve
to can	[kən]	können
candle	[ˈkædl]	Kerze
canoe	[kəˈnuː]	Kanu
cap	[kæp]	Kappe
car	[kaː(r)]	Auto
carnation	[kaːˈneɪʃn]	Nelke
carpark	[ˈkaːpaːk]	Parkplatz
carpenter	[ˈkaːpəntə(r)]	Schreiner
carrot	[ˈkærət]	Karotte
to carry	[ˈkærɪ]	tragen
cassette	[kəˈset]	Kassette
cassette player	[kəˈsetˈpleiə(r)]	Kassettenrecorder
castle	[ˈkaːsl]	Schloß
cat	[kæt]	Katze
to catch	[kætʃ]	fangen
caterpillar	[ˈkætəpɪlə(r)]	Raupe
cattle	[ˈkætl]	Rind
cauliflower	[ˈkɒlɪflaʊə(r)]	Blumenkohl
cave	[keɪv]	Höhle
CD (compact disc)	[ˌsiːdiː]	CD
CD-ROM	[ˌsiːdiːˈrɒm]	CD-ROM
ceiling	[ˈsiːlɪŋ]	Decke
centipede	[ˈsentɪpiːd]	Tausendfüßer
cereal	[ˈsɪərɪəl]	Getreide
chair	[tʃeə(r)]	Stuhl
chameleon	[kəˈmiːlɪən]	Chamäleon
champion	[ˈtʃæmpɪən]	Champion
to chase	[tʃeɪs]	jagen
cheap	[tʃiːp]	billig
checkout	[tʃekaʊt]	Kasse
to cheer	[tʃɪə(r)]	jubeln
cheese	[tʃiːz]	Käse
cheetah	[ˈtʃiːtə]	Gepard
chess	[tʃes]	Schach
chest	[tʃest]	Brust
chest of drawers	[tʃest ɒv drɔː(r)s]	Kommode
chick	[tʃɪk]	Küken
chicken	[ˈtʃɪkɪn]	Huhn
child	[tʃaɪld]	Kind
children	[ˈtʃɪldrən]	Kinder
chimney	[ˈtʃɪmnɪ]	Kamin
chimpanzee	[ˌtʃɪmpænˈziː]	Schimpanse
chin	[tʃɪn]	Kinn
chocolate	[ˈtʃɒklət]	Schokolade
choir	[ˈkwaɪə(r)]	Chor
to choose	[tʃuːz]	auswählen
chop-sticks	[tʃɒpstɪks]	Stäbchen
church	[tʃɜːtʃ]	Kirche
cinema	[ˈsɪnəmə]	Kino
circle	[ˈsɜːkl]	Kreis
city	[ˈsɪtɪ]	Stadt
to clap	[klæp]	klatschen
claw	[klɔː]	Klaue
clean	[kliːn]	sauber
cliff	[klɪf]	Klippe
to climb	[klaɪm]	klettern
clock	[klɒk]	Uhr
to close	[kləʊs]	schließen
clothes	[kləʊðz]	Kleider
cloud	[klaʊd]	Wolke
clown	[klaʊn]	Clown
coat	[kəʊt]	Mantel
cobweb	[ˈkɒbweb]	Spinnennetz
cockerel	[ˈkɒkərəl]	Gockel
cockpit	[ˈkɒkpɪt]	Cockpit
coconut	[ˈkəʊkəʊnʌt]	Kokosnuss
coffee	[ˈkɒfɪ]	Kaffee
cold	[kəʊld]	kalt
colour	[ˈkʌlə(r)]	Farbe
to colour	[ˈkʌlə(r)]	färben
to come	[kʌm]	kommen
compact disc	[kəmˈpæktdɪsk]	CD
computer	[kəmˈpjuːtə(r)]	Computer
conductor	[kənˈdʌktə(r)]	Dirigent
cone	[kəʊn]	Kegel
continent	[ˈkɒntɪnənt]	Kontinent
to cook	[kʊk]	kochen
corner	[ˈkɔːnə(r)]	Ecke
cotton	[ˈkɒtn]	Baumwolle
to count	[kaʊnt]	zählen
country	[ˈkʌntrɪ]	Land
cousin	[ˈkʌzn]	Cousin/Cousine
cow	[kaʊ]	Kuh
crab	[kræb]	Krabbe
crane	[kreɪn]	Kran
to crawl	[krɔːl]	krabbeln
crayon	[ˈkreɪən]	Buntstift
cricket	[ˈkrɪkɪt]	Kricket
cricket	[ˈkrɪkɪt]	Grille
crocodile	[ˈkrɒkədaɪl]	Krokodil
crow	[krəʊ]	Krähe
crowd	[kraʊd]	Menge
crown	[kraʊn]	Krone
crutch	[krʌtʃ]	Krücke
to cry	[kraɪ]	weinen
cube	[kjuːb]	Würfel
cucumber	[ˈkjuːkʌmbə(r)]	Gurke
cup	[kʌp]	Tasse
cupboard	[ˈkʌbəd]	Schrank
curtain	[ˈkɜːtn]	Vorhang
cushion	[ˈkʊʃn]	Kissen
to cut	[kʌt]	schneiden

D (Seite 21–25)

daffodil	[ˈdæfədɪl]	Osterglocke
daisy	[ˈdeɪzɪ]	Gänseblümchen
dam	[dæm]	Damm
to dance	[daːns]	tanzen
dandelion	[ˈdændɪlaɪən]	Löwenzahn
daughter	[ˈdɔːtə(r)]	Tochter
day	[deɪ]	Tag
deaf	[def]	taub
december	[dɪˈsembə(r)]	Dezember
deer	[dɪə(r)]	Hirsch
dentist	[ˈdentɪst]	Zahnarzt

desert	[ˈdezət]	Wüste
desk	[desk]	Schreibtisch
dessert	[dɪˈzɜːt]	Nachtisch
detective	[dɪˈtektɪv]	Detektiv
diagram	[ˈdaɪəɡræm]	Diagramm
diamond	[ˈdaɪəmənd]	Diamant
diary	[ˈdaɪəri]	Tagebuch
dictionary	[ˈdɪkʃənri]	Wörterbuch
different	[ˈdɪfrənt]	verschieden
dinner	[ˈdɪnə(r)]	Abendessen
dinosaur	[ˈdaɪnəsɔː(r)]	Dinosaurier
dirty	[ˈdɜːti]	schmutzig
disguise	[dɪsˈɡaɪz]	Verkleidung
to dive	[daɪv]	springen, tauchen
diver	[ˈdaɪvə(r)]	Taucher
doctor	[ˈdɒktə(r)]	Doktor
to do	[duː]	tun
doe	[dəʊ]	Hirschkuh
dog	[dɒɡ]	Hund
doll	[dɒl]	Puppe
dolphin	[ˈdɒlfɪn]	Delfin
donkey	[ˈdɒŋki]	Esel
door	[dɔːr]	Türe
double	[ˈdʌbl]	doppelt
down	[daʊn]	hinunter
dragon	[ˈdræɡən]	Drache
dragonfly	[ˈdræɡənflaɪ]	Libelle
drake	[dreɪk]	Erpel
to draw	[drɔː]	zeichnen
drawer	[ˈdrɔː(r)]	Schublade
dress	[dres]	Kleid
to dress	[dres]	anziehen
to drill	[drɪl]	bohren
to drink	[ˈdrɪŋk]	trinken
to drive	[draɪv]	fahren
driver	[ˈdraɪvə(r)]	Fahrer
to drop	[drɒp]	fallen lassen
drum	[drʌm]	Trommel
drumstick	[ˈdrʌmstɪk]	Trommelschlegel
to dry	[draɪ]	trocknen
duck	[dʌk]	Ente
duckling	[ˈdʌklɪŋ]	Entenküken
dumper truck	[ˈdʌmpə(r) trʌk]	Kipper

E (Seite 25–27)

eagle	[ˈiːɡl]	Adler
ear	[ɪə(r)]	Ohr
Earth	[ɜːθ]	Erde
easel	[ˈiːzl]	Staffelei
eat	[iːt]	Essen
egg	[eɡ]	Ei
eight	[eɪt]	acht
elbow	[ˈelbəʊ]	Ellbogen
electricity	[ɪˌlekˈtrɪsəti]	Elektrizität
elephant	[ˈelɪfənt]	Elefant
empty	[ˈempti]	leer
emu	[ˈiːmjuː]	Emu
engine	[ˈendʒɪn]	Maschine
engineer	[ˌendʒɪˈnɪə(r)]	Ingenieur
enter	[ˈentə(r)]	betreten
entrance	[ˈentrəns]	Eingang
equal	[ˈiːkwəl]	gleich
equator	[ɪˈkweɪtə(r)]	Äquator
escalator	[ˈeskəleɪtə(r)]	Rolltreppe
Europe	[ˈjʊərəp]	Europa
evening	[ˈiːvnɪŋ]	Abend
ewe	[juː]	Mutterschaf
to exercise	[ˈeksəsaɪz]	üben
exit	[ˈeksɪt]	Ausgang
expensive	[ɪkˈspensɪv]	teuer
to explode	[ɪkˈspləʊd]	explodieren
eye	[aɪ]	Auge
eyebrow	[ˈaɪbraʊ]	Augenbraue

F (Seite 28–32)

face	[feɪs]	Gesicht
factory	[ˈfæktəri]	Fabrik
fair	[ˈfeə(r)]	Messe
to fall	[fɔːl]	fallen
family	[ˈfæməli]	Familie
fan	[fæn]	Fächer
farm	[faːm]	Bauernhof
farmer	[ˈfaːmə(r)]	Bauer
fast	[faːst]	schnell
fat	[fæt]	dick
father	[ˈfaːðə(r)]	Vater
fawn	[fɔːn]	Hirschkalb
feather	[ˈfeðə(r)]	Feder
to feed	[fiːd]	ernähren
female	[ˈfiːmeɪl]	weiblich
fight	[faɪt]	Kampf
film	[fɪlm]	Film
finger	[ˈfɪŋɡə(r)]	Finger
fingerprint	[ˈfɪŋɡəprɪnt]	Fingerabdruck
to finish	[ˈfɪnɪʃ]	beenden
fire	[ˈfaɪə(r)]	Feuer
fire engine	[ˈfaɪəˈendʒɪn]	Feuerwehrauto
fire fighter	[ˈfaɪəˈfaɪtə(r)]	Feuerwehrmann
first aid	[fɜːstˌeɪd]	Erste Hilfe
fish	[fɪʃ]	Fisch
to fish	[fɪʃ]	fischen
five	[faɪv]	fünf
flag	[flæɡ]	Flagge
flipper	[ˈflɪpə(r)]	Flosse
to float	[fləʊt]	treiben
flood	[flʌd]	Überschwemmung
floor	[flɔː(r)]	Boden
flour	[ˈflaʊə(r)]	Mehl
flower	[ˈflaʊə(r)]	Blume
flute	[fluːt]	Flöte
to fly	[flaɪ]	fliegen
fly	[flaɪ]	Fliege
foal	[fəʊl]	Fohlen
fog	[fɒɡ]	Nebel
to fold	[fəʊld]	falten
food	[fuːd]	Essen
foot	[fʊt]	Fuß
football	[ˈfʊtbɔːl]	Fußball
footprint	[ˈfʊtprɪnt]	Fußabdruck
forehead	[ˈfɒrɪd]	Stirn
forest	[ˈfɒrɪst]	Wald
fork	[fɔːk]	Gabel
fossil	[ˈfɒsl]	Fossil
fountain	[ˈfaʊntɪn]	Springbrunnen
four	[fɔː(r)]	vier
fox	[fɒks]	Fuchs
France	[fraːns]	Frankreich
Friday	[ˈfraɪdɪ]	Freitag
friend	[frend]	Freund
frog	[frɒɡ]	Frosch
fruit	[fruːt]	Frucht
frying-pan	[ˈfraɪŋpæn]	Pfanne
full	[fʊl]	voll
fur	[fɜː(r)]	Pelz
furniture	[ˈfɜːnɪtʃə(r)]	Möbel

G (Seite 32–34)

game	[ɡeɪm]	Spiel
gander	[ˈɡændə(r)]	Gänserich
garage	[ˈɡæraːʒ, ɡəˈraːʒ]	Garage

A B C D E F G H I J K L M N O P Q R S T U V W X Y Z

garden	[ˈgɑːdn]	Garten
gate	[geɪt]	Tor
geese	[giːs]	Gänse
to get	[get]	bekommen
ghost	[gəʊst]	Geist
giant	[ˈdʒaɪənt]	Riese
giraffe	[dʒɪˈrɑːf]	Giraffe
girl	[gɜːl]	Mädchen
to give	[gɪv]	geben
glass	[glɑːs]	Glas
glasses	[glɑːsɪz]	Brille
globe	[gləʊb]	Globus
glove	[glʌv]	Handschuh
glue	[gluː]	Klebstoff
to go	[gəʊ]	gehen
goal	[gəʊl]	Tor
goat	[gəʊt]	Ziege
goggles	[gɒglz]	Schwimmbrille
gold	[gəʊld]	Gold
goldfish	[gəʊldfɪʃ]	Goldfisch
golf	[gɒlf]	Golf
goose	[guːs]	Gans
gorilla	[gəˈrɪlə]	Gorilla
gosling	[ˈgɒzlɪŋ]	Gänseküken
grandchildren	[ˈgrændˌʃɪldrən]	Enkelkinder
grandfather	[ˈgrændˌfɑːðə(r)]	Großvater
grandmother	[ˈgrændˌmʌðə(r)]	Großmutter
grandparent	[ˈgrændˌpeərənt]	Großelternteil
grape	[greɪp]	Weintraube
grapefruit	[ˈgreɪpfruːt]	Grapefruit
grass	[grɑːs]	Gras
grasshopper	[ˈgrɑːshɒpə(r)]	Heuschrecke
green	[griːn]	grün
to grow	[grəʊ]	wachsen
guide dog	[gaɪdˌdɒg]	Blindenhund
guitar	[gɪˈtɑː(r)]	Gitarre
gymnasium	[dʒɪmˈneɪzɪəm]	Turnhalle
gymnast	[ˈdʒɪmnæst]	Turner

H (Seite 35–38)

hair	[heə(r)]	Haare
hair-brush	[ˈheəbrʌʃ]	Haarbürste
half	[hɑːf]	halb
halves	[hɑːvs]	Hälften
hammer	[ˈhæmə(r)]	Hammer
hand	[hænd]	Hand
handle	[ˈhændl]	Griff
handlebar	[ˈhændlbɑː]	Lenkstange
to hang	[hæŋ]	hängen
hangar	[ˈhæŋə(r)]	Hangar
happy	[ˈhæpɪ]	glücklich
harbour	[ˈhɑːbə(r)]	Hafen
hat	[hæt]	Hut
hate	[heɪt]	hassen
to have	[həv]	haben
hawk	[hɔːk]	Habicht
head	[hed]	Kopf
headlamp	[ˈhedlæmp]	Scheinwerfer
hearing-aid	[ˈhɪərɪŋˌeɪd]	Hörgerät
heart	[hɑːt]	Herz
heavy	[ˈhevɪ]	schwer
heel	[hɪːl]	Ferse
helicopter	[ˈhelɪkɒptə(r)]	Hubschrauber
helmet	[ˈhelmɪt]	Helm
to help	[help]	helfen
hen	[hen]	Henne
hibernate	[ˈhaɪbəneɪt]	Winterschlaf halten
to hide	[haɪd]	verstecken
high	[haɪ]	hoch
hill	[hɪl]	Hügel
hip	[hɪp]	Hüfte
hippopotamus	[ˌhɪpəˈpɒtəməs]	Nilpferd
to hold	[həʊld]	halten
hole	[həʊl]	Loch
honey	[ˈhʌnɪ]	Honig
hoof	[huːf]	Hufe
to hop	[hɒp]	hüpfen
horn	[hɔːn]	Hupe
horse	[hɔːs]	Pferd
hospital	[ˈhɒspɪtl]	Krankenhaus
hot	[hɒt]	heiß
hotel	[həʊˈtel]	Hotel
hour	[ˈaʊə(r)]	Stunde
house	[haʊs]	Haus
hug	[hʌg]	Umarmung
hundred	[ˈhʌndrəd]	Hundert
husband	[ˈhʌzbənd]	Ehemann
hutch	[hʌtʃ]	Kaninchenstall
hyena	[haɪˈiːnə]	Hyäne

I (Seite 38–39)

ice	[aɪs]	Eis
iceberg	[ˈaɪsbɜːg]	Eisberg
ice-cream	[ˈaɪskriːm]	Eis(creme)
ice skates	[ˈaɪskeɪts]	Schlittschuhe
icicle	[ˈaɪsɪkl]	Eiszapfen
igloo	[ˈɪgluː]	Iglu
iguana	[ɪˈgwɑːnə]	Leguan
indigo	[ˈɪndɪˌgoʊ]	indigo
injection	[ɪnˈdʒekʃn]	Spritze
to injure	[ˈɪndʒə(r)]	verletzen
injury	[ˈɪndʒərɪ]	Verletzung
insect	[ˈɪnsekt]	Insekt
inside	[ɪnˈsaɪd]	innen
instrument	[ˈɪnstrʊmənt]	Instrument
to invent	[ɪnˈvent]	erfinden
inventor	[ɪnˈventə(r)]	Erfinder
invitation	[ˌɪnvɪˈteɪʃn]	Einladung
to invite	[ɪnˈvaɪt]	einladen
iron	[ˈaɪən]	Eisen
is	[ɪs]	(er) ist
island	[ˈaɪlənd]	Insel
ivy	[ˈaɪvɪ]	Efeu

J (Seite 40–41)

jacket	[ˈdʒækɪt]	Jacke
jaguar	[ˈdʒægjʊə(r)]	Jaguar
jam	[dʒæm]	Marmelade
january	[ˈdʒænjʊərɪ]	Januar
jar	[dʒɑː(r)]	Einmachglas
jaw	[dʒɔː]	Kiefer
jeans	[dʒiːnz]	Jeans
jellyfish	[ˈdʒelɪfɪʃ]	Qualle
jewel	[ˈdʒuːəl]	Edelstein
jewellery	[ˈdʒuːəlrɪ]	Juwelen
jigsaw / puzzle	[ˈdʒɪgsɔː] [ˈpʌzl]	Puzzle
judo	[ˈdʒuːdəʊ]	Judo
jug	[dʒʌg]	Krug
to juggle	[ˈdʒʌgl]	jonglieren
juggler	[ˈdʒʌglə(r)]	Jongleur
juice	[dʒuːs]	Saft
July	[dʒuːˈlaɪ]	Juli
to jump	[dʒʌmp]	springen
June	[dʒuːn]	Juni
jungle	[ˈdʒʌŋgl]	Dschungel
jupiter	[ˈdʒuːpɪtə(r)]	Jupiter

K (Seite 41–42)

kangaroo	[ˌkæŋgəˈruː]	Känguru
karate	[kəˈrɑːtɪ]	Karate

A B C D E F G H I J K L M N O P Q R S T U V W X Y Z

kennel	[ˈkenl]	Hundehütte		magnet	[ˈmægnɪt]	Magnet
key	[kiː]	Schlüssel		magnifying glass	[ˈmægnɪfaɪŋ glaːs]	Lupe
kick	[kik]	Fußtritt		to make	[ˈmeɪk]	machen
kid	[kid]	Zicklein, Kind		male	[meɪl]	männlich
king	[kiŋ]	König		mammal	[ˈmæml]	Säugetier
to kiss	[kis]	küssen		man	[mæn]	Mann
kitchen	[ˈkɪtʃɪn]	Küche		March	[maːtʃ]	März
kite	[kait]	Drachen		market	[ˈmaːkɪt]	Markt
kitten	[ˈkɪtn]	Kätzchen		mask	[maːsk]	Maske
knee	[niː]	Knie		match	[mætʃ]	Streichholz
to kneel	[niːl]	knien		mathematics	[ˌmæθəˈmætɪks]	Mathematik
knife	[naɪf]	Messer		May	[meɪ]	Mai
knight	[naɪt]	Ritter		meal	[miːl]	Mahlzeit
to knit	[nɪt]	stricken		to measure	[ˈmeʒə(r)]	messen
to knock	[nɒk]	klopfen		meat	[miːt]	Fleisch
knot	[nɒt]	Knoten		mechanic	[mɪˈkænɪk]	Mechaniker
koala	[kəʊˈaːlə]	Koala		medal	[ˈmedl]	Medaille
				medicine	[ˈmedsn]	Medikament
L (Seite 43–46)				to meet	[miːt]	treffen
laboratory	[ləˈbɒrətrɪ]	Labor		to melt	[melt]	schmelzen
ladder	[ˈlædə(r)]	Leiter		men	[men]	Männer
ladybird	[ˈleɪdɪbɜːd]	Marienkäfer		Mercury	[ˈmɜːkjʊrɪ]	Merkur
lake	[leɪk]	See		metal	[ˈmetl]	Metall
lamb	[læm]	Lamm		mice	[maɪs]	Mäuse
lamp	[læmp]	Lampe		microphone	[ˈmaɪkrəfəʊn]	Mikrofon
land	[lænd]	Festland		microscope	[ˈmaɪkrəskəʊp]	Mikroskop
large	[laːdʒ]	groß		microwave oven	[ˈmaɪkrəʊweɪvˌʌvn]	Mikrowellenherd
to laugh	[laːf]	lachen		midday	[ˌmɪdˈdeɪ]	Mittag
lawn	[lɔːn]	Rasen		milk	[mɪlk]	Milch
lawnmower	[ˈlɔːnˌməʊə(r)]	Rasenmäher		mine	[maɪn]	Mine
leaf	[liːf]	Blatt		mineral	[ˈmɪnərəl]	Mineral
to lean	[liːn]	lehnen		minute	[ˈmɪnɪt]	Minute
left	[left]	links		mirror	[ˈmɪrə(r)]	Spiegel
leg	[leg]	Fuß		to mix	[mɪks]	mischen
lemon	[ˈlemən]	Limone		Monday	[ˈmʌndɪ]	Montag
leopard	[ˈlepəd]	Leopard		money	[ˈmʌnɪ]	Geld
letter	[ˈletə(r)]	Buchstabe		monkey	[ˈmʌŋkɪ]	Affe
letter	[ˈletə(r)]	Brief		monster	[ˈmɒnstə(r)]	Ungeheuer
lettuce	[ˈletɪs]	Kopfsalat		month	[mʌnθ]	Monat
library	[ˈlaɪbrərɪ]	Bücherei		moon	[muːn]	Mond
to lick	[lɪk]	lecken		morning	[ˈmɔːnɪŋ]	Morgen
lifeboat	[ˈlaɪfbəʊt]	Rettungsboot		mosaic	[məʊˈzeɪɪk]	Mosaik
lightning	[ˈlaɪtnɪŋ]	Blitz		mosque	[mɒsk]	Moschee
to like	[laɪk]	mögen		mosquito	[məˈskiːtəʊ]	Mücke
lion	[ˈlaɪən]	Löwe		moth	[mɒθ]	Nachtfalter
lioness	[laɪəˈnes]	Löwin		mother	[ˈmʌðə(r)]	Mutter
lip	[lɪp]	Lippe		mouth	[maʊθ]	Mund
liquid	[ˈlɪkwɪd]	Flüssigkeit		mud	[mʌd]	Schlamm
to listen	[ˈlɪsn]	zuhören		muscle	[ˈmʌsl]	Muskel
litter	[ˈlɪtə(r)]	Abfall		museum	[mjuːˈzɪəm]	Museum
little	[ˈlɪtl]	klein		mushroom	[ˈmʌʃrʊm]	Pilz
to live	[lɪv]	leben		music	[ˈmjuːˈzɪk]	Musik
lizard	[ˈlɪzəd]	Eidechse		musician	[mjuːˈzɪʃn]	Musiker
lobster	[ˈlɒbstə(r)]	Hummer		to must	[mʌst]	müssen
lock	[lɒk]	Schloß				
log	[lɒg]	Holzklotz		**N** (Seite 51–52)		
long	[lɒŋ]	lang		nail	[neɪl]	Fingernagel
to look	[lʊk]	sehen		nanny goat	[ˈnænɪgəʊt]	Geiß
to lose	[luːz]	verlieren		narrow	[ˈnærəʊ]	eng
to love	[lʌv]	lieben		navy	[ˈneɪvɪ]	Flotte
low	[ləʊ]	niedrig		neck	[nek]	Nacken
luggage	[ˈlʌgɪdʒ]	Gepäck		needle	[ˈniːdl]	Nadel
lunch	[lʌntʃ]	Mittagessen		nest	[nest]	Nest
lung	[lʌŋ]	Lunge		net	[net]	Netz
				new	[njuː]	neu
M (Seite 46–51)				newspaper	[ˈnjuːspeɪpə(r)]	Zeitung
machine	[məˈʃiːn]	Maschine		newt	[njuːt]	Molch
magazine	[ˌmægəˈziːn]	Zeitschrift		night	[naɪt]	Nacht
magic	[ˈmædʒɪk]	Zauberei		nine	[naɪn]	neun
magician	[məˈdʒɪʃn]	Zauberer		noise	[nɔɪz]	Lärm

A B C D E F G H I J K L M N O P Q R S T U V W X Y Z

North America	[ɔː(r)θ əˈmerikə]	Nordamerika
nose	[nəʊz]	Nase
number	[ˈnʌmbə(r)]	Nummer
nurse	[nɜːs]	Krankenschwester
nut	[nʌt]	(Schrauben)Mutter
nut	[nʌt]	Nuss
nutcracker	[ˈnʌtˌkrækə(r)]	Nussknacker

O (Seite 53–54)

oar	[ɔː(r)]	Ruder
oat	[əʊt]	Hafer
ocean	[ˈəʊʃn]	Ozean
october	[ɒkˈtəʊbə(r)]	Oktober
octopus	[ˈɒktəpəs]	Tintenfisch
office	[ˈɒfɪs]	Büro
oil	[ɔɪl]	Öl
old	[əʊld]	alt
one	[wʌn]	eins
onion	[ˈʌnɪən]	Zwiebel
open	[ˈəʊpən]	offen
to open	[ˈəʊpən]	öffnen
opera	[ˈɒprə]	Oper
opposite	[ˈɒpəzɪt]	gegenteilig
optician	[ɒpˈtɪʃn]	Optiker
orange	[ˈɒrɪndʒ]	orange(farben)
orange	[ˈɒrɪndʒ]	Orange
orang-utan	[ɔːˈræŋuːˈtæn]	Orang-Utan
orchard	[ˈɔːtʃəd]	Obstgarten
orchestra	[ˈɔːkɪstrə]	Orchester
organ	[ˈɔːɡən]	Orgel
ostrich	[ˈɒstrɪʃ]	Strauß
otter	[ˈɒtə(r)]	Otter
outside	[ˌaʊtˈsaɪd]	außen
oval	[ˈəʊvl]	oval
oven	[ˈʌvn]	Ofen
owl	[əʊl]	Eule
oyster	[ˈɔɪstə(r)]	Auster

P (Seite 55–63)

page	[peɪdʒ]	Seite
to paint	[peɪnt]	malen
pair	[peə(r)]	Paar
palace	[ˈpælɪs]	Palast
palm	[paːm]	Handfläche
palm tree	[paːmtriː]	Palme
panda	[ˈpændə]	Panda-Bär
panther	[ˈpænθə(r)]	Panther
paper	[ˈpeɪpə(r)]	Papier
parachute	[ˈpærəʃuːt]	Fallschirm
parcel	[ˈpaːsl]	Paket
parent	[ˈpeərənt]	Elternteil
park	[paːk]	Park
parrot	[ˈpærət]	Papagei
party	[ˈpaːtɪ]	Fest
to pass	[paːs]	vorbeigehen
passenger	[ˈpæsɪndʒə(r)]	Passagier
path	[ˈpaːθ]	Fußweg
patient	[ˈpeɪʃnt]	Patient
paw	[pɔː]	Pfote
to pay	[peɪ]	zahlen
pea	[piː]	Erbse
peach	[piːtʃ]	Pfirsich
peacock	[ˈpiːkɒk]	Pfau
peanut	[ˈpiːnʌt]	Erdnuss
pear	[peə(r)]	Birne
pearl	[pɜːl]	Perle
pebble	[ˈpebl]	Kiesel
pedal	[ˈpedl]	Pedal
peel	[piːl]	Schale
to peel	[piːl]	schälen
pelican	[ˈpelɪkən]	Pelikan
pen	[pen]	Federhalter
pencil	[ˈpensl]	Bleistift
penguin	[ˈpeŋgwɪn]	Pinguine
people	[ˈpiːpl]	Menschen
pepper	[ˈpepə(r)]	Pfeffer
perfume	[ˈpɜːfjuːm]	Parfüm
pet	[pet]	Haustier
petal	[ˈpetl]	Blütenblatt
photograph	[ˈfəʊtəgraːf]	Fotographie
photographer	[fəʊˈtɒgrəfə(r)]	Fotograph
piano	[ˈpjaːnəʊ]	Klavier
picnic	[ˈpɪknɪk]	Picknick
picture	[ˈpɪktʃə(r)]	Bild
pie	[paɪ]	Teigtasche
pig	[pɪg]	Schwein
pigeon	[ˈpɪdʒɪn]	Taube
piglet	[ˈpɪglɪt]	Ferkel
pile	[paɪl]	Haufen
pillow	[ˈpɪləʊ]	Kissen
pilot	[ˈpaɪlət]	Pilot
pin	[pɪn]	Stecknadel
pineapple	[ˈpaɪnæpl]	Ananas
pink	[pɪŋk]	rosa
pipe	[paɪp]	Rohr
pirate	[ˈpaɪərət]	Pirat
planet	[ˈplænɪt]	Planet
plant	[plaːnt]	Pflanze
plastic	[ˈplæstɪk]	Plastik
plate	[pleɪt]	Teller
play	[pleɪ]	spielen
plum	[plʌm]	Pflaume
plumber	[ˈplʌmə(r)]	Klempner
Pluto	[ˈpluːtə]	Pluto
pocket	[ˈpɒkɪt]	Tasche
point	[pɔɪnt]	Spitze
polar bear	[ˈpəʊlərbeə(r)]	Eisbär
police officer	[pəˈliːsˌɒfɪsə(r)]	Polizist
polish	[ˈpɒlɪʃ]	polieren
pond	[pɒnd]	Teich
pony	[ˈpəʊnɪ]	Pony
poppy	[ˈpɒpɪ]	Mohnblume
porcubine	[ˈpɔːkjʊpaɪn]	Stachelschwein
post office	[ˈpəʊstˌɒfɪs]	Postamt
postal worker	[ˈpəʊstlˌwɜːkə(r)]	Postbeamter
potato	[pəˈteɪtəʊ]	Kartoffel
to pour	[pɔː(r)]	gießen
prawn	[prɔːn]	Garnele
present	[ˈpreznt]	Geschenk
price	[praɪs]	Preis
prickle	[ˈprɪkl]	Stachel
prince	[prɪns]	Prinz
princess	[prɪnˈses]	Prinzessin
prize	[praɪz]	Preis
propeller	[prəˈpelə(r)]	Propeller
puddle	[ˈpʌdl]	Pfütze
to pull	[pʊl]	ziehen
pump	[pʌmp]	Pumpe
puncture	[ˈpʌŋktʃə(r)]	Loch
pupa	[ˈpjuːpə]	Puppe, Schmetterling
puppet	[ˈpʌpɪt]	Marionette
puppy	[ˈpʌpɪ]	Welpen
purple	[ˈpɜːpl]	purpur
to push	[pʊʃ]	schieben
to put	[pʊt]	legen
puzzle	[ˈpʌzl]	Rätsel
pyramid	[ˈpɪrəmɪd]	Pyramide
python	[ˈpaɪθən]	Python

A B C D E F G H I J K L M N O P Q R S T U V W X Y Z

Q (Seite 63)
quarry	[ˈkwɒrɪ]	Steinbruch
quarter	[ˈkwɔːtə(r)]	Viertel
queen	[kwiːn]	Königin
quick	[kwɪk]	schnell
quiet	[ˈkwaɪət]	ruhig
quilt	[kwɪlt]	Steppdecke
quiz	[kwɪz]	Quiz

R (Seite 64–67)
rabbit	[ˈræbɪt]	Kaninchen
race	[reɪs]	Rennen
racing car	[ˈreɪsɪŋˌkaː(r)]	Rennauto
radio	[ˈreɪdɪəʊ]	Radio
raft	[raːft]	Floß
rail	[reɪl]	Gleis
railway	[ˈreɪlweɪ]	Eisenbahn
railway station	[ˈreɪlweɪˌsteɪʃn]	Bahnhof
rain	[reɪn]	Regen
to rain	[reɪn]	regnen
rainbow	[ˈreɪnbəʊ]	Regenbogen
rainforest	[ˈreɪnfɒrɪst]	Regenwald
to reach	[riːtʃ]	erreichen
to read	[riːd]	lesen
record	[ˈrekɔːd]	Schallplatte
recorder	[rɪˈkɔːdə(r)]	Blockflöte
record player	[ˈrekɔːdˌpleɪə(r)]	Plattenspieler
rectangle	[ˈrektæŋgl]	Rechteck
red	[red]	rot
refrigerator	[rɪˈfrɪdʒəˌreɪtə(r)]	Kühlschrank
to repair	[rɪˈpeə(r)]	reparieren
reptile	[ˈreptaɪl]	Reptil
to rescue	[ˈreskjuː]	retten
restaurant	[ˈrestrɒnt]	Restaurant
rhinoceros	[raɪˈnɒsərəs]	Nashorn
ribbon	[ˈrɪbən]	Band
rice	[raɪs]	Reis
to ride	[raɪd]	reiten
right	[raɪt]	rechts
ring	[rɪŋ]	Ring
to ring	[rɪŋ]	klingeln
river	[ˈrɪvə(r)]	Fluss
road	[rəʊd]	Straße
robot	[ˈrəʊbɒt]	Roboter
rock	[rɒk]	Felsen
rocket	[ˈrɒkɪt]	Rakete
to roll	[rəʊl]	rollen
roof	[ruːf]	Dach
room	[ruːm]	Zimmer
root	[ruːt]	Wurzel
rope	[rəʊp]	Seil
rose	[rəʊz]	Rose
round	[raʊnd]	rund
row	[rəʊ]	Reihe
rug	[rʌg]	Vorlegeteppich
ruler	[ˈruːlə(r)]	Lineal
runway	[ˈrʌnweɪ]	Landebahn
rye	[raɪ]	Roggen

S (Seite 68–77)
sad	[sæd]	traurig
saddle	[ˈsædl]	Sattel
sail	[seɪl]	Segel
to sail	[seɪl]	segeln
sailing boat	[ˈseɪlɪŋˌbəʊt]	Segelboot
sailor	[ˈseɪlə(r)]	Segler
salad	[ˈsæləd]	Salat
salt	[sɔːlt]	Salz
same	[seɪm]	gleich
sand	[sænd]	Sand
sandwich	[ˈsændwɪdʒ]	Sandwich
satellite	[ˈsætəˌlaɪt]	Satellit
satellite dish	[ˈsætəlaɪtˌdɪʃ]	Satellitenschüssel
saucepan	[ˈsɔːspən]	Kochtopf
saturday	[ˈsætədɪ]	Samstag
Saturn	[ˈsætən]	Saturn
saw	[sɔː]	Säge
to say	[seɪ]	sagen
scale	[skeɪl]	Schuppe
scales	[skeɪls]	Waage
scarf	[scaːf]	Schal
school	[skuːl]	Schule
scientist	[ˈsaɪəntɪst]	Wissenschaftler
scissors	[ˈsɪzəz]	Schere
scorpion	[ˈskɔːpɪən]	Skorpion
to scratch	[skrætʃ]	kratzen
screw	[skruː]	Schraube
to scrub	[skrʌb]	schrubben
sea	[siː]	Meer
seagull	[ˈsiːgʌl]	Möwe
seahorse	[ˈsiːhɔːs]	Seepferd
seal	[siːl]	Seehund
season	[ˈsiːzn]	Jahreszeit
seat	[siːt]	Sitz
seat-belt	[siːtˌbelt]	Gurt
seaweed	[ˈsiːwiːd]	Seetang
second	[ˈsekənd]	Sekunde
to see	[siː]	sehen
seed	[siːd]	Samen
seesaw	[ˈsiːsɔː]	Wippe
to sell	[sel]	verkaufen
to send	[send]	senden
seven	[ˈsevn]	sieben
to sew	[səʊ]	nähen
shadow	[ˈʃædəʊ]	Schatten
to shake	[ʃeɪk]	schütteln
shape	[ʃeɪp]	Form
to share	[ʃeə(r)]	teilen
shark	[ʃaːk]	Hai
sharp	[ʃaːp]	scharf
sheep	[ʃiːp]	Schaf
shelf	[ʃelf]	Regal
shell	[ʃel]	Schale
ship	[ʃɪp]	Schiff
shirt	[ʃɜːt]	Hemd
shoe	[ʃuː]	Schuh
shop	[ʃɒp]	Laden
short	[ʃɔːt]	kurz
shoulder	[ˈʃəʊldə(r)]	Schulter
shout	[ʃaʊt]	schreien
show	[ʃaʊ]	zeigen
shower	[ˈʃaʊə(r)]	Dusche
to shut	[ʃʌt]	schließen
to sing	[sɪŋ]	singen
to sink	[sɪŋk]	sinken
sister	[ˈsɪstə(r)]	Schwester
to sit	[sɪt]	sitzen
six	[sɪks]	sechs
to skate	[skeɪt]	Schlittschuhlaufen
skeleton	[ˈskelɪtn]	Skelett
ski	[skiː]	Ski
to skip	[skɪp]	seilhüpfen
skipping-rope	[ˈskɪpɪŋrəʊp]	Springseil
skirt	[skɜːt]	Rock
sky	[skaɪ]	Himmel
skyscraper	[ˈskaɪskreɪpə(r)]	Wolkenkratzer
sledge	[sledʒ]	Schlitten
sleep	[sliːp]	schlafen
slice	[slaɪs]	Scheibe

A B C D E F G H I J K L M N O P Q R S T U V W X Y Z

slide	[slaɪd]	Rutschbahn		teacher	[ˈtiːtʃə(r)]	Lehrer
slow	[sləʊ]	langsam		team	[tiːm]	Mannschaft, Team
small	[smɔːl]	klein		tear	[tɪ(r)]	Träne
to smile	[smaɪl]	lächeln		to tear	[tɪ(r)]	zerreißen
snail	[sneɪl]	Schnecke		teeth	[tiːθ]	Zähne
snake	[sneɪk]	Schlange		telephone	[ˈtelɪfəʊn]	Telefon
snow	[snəʊ]	Schnee		telescope	[ˈtelɪskəʊp]	Fernrohr
snowman	[ˈsnəʊmæn]	Schneemann		television	[ˈtelɪˌvɪʒn]	Fernsehen
soap	[səʊp]	Seife		temperature	[ˈtemprətʃə(r)]	Temperatur
soccer	[ˈsɒkə(r)]	Fußball		temple	[ˈtempl]	Tempel
sock	[sɒk]	Socke		ten	[ten]	zehn
sofa	[ˈsəʊfə]	Sofa		tennis	[ˈtenɪs]	Tennis
soldier	[ˈsəʊldʒə(r)]	Soldat		tent	[tent]	Zelt
solid	[ˈsɒlɪd]	fest		to thank	[θæŋk]	danken
son	[sʌn]	Sohn		theatre	[ˈθɪətə(r)]	Theater
South America	[ˈsaʊθ əˈmerɪkə]	Südamerika		thermometer	[θəˈmɒmɪtə(r)]	Thermometer
sow	[saʊ]	Sau, (Mutter)Schwein		thigh	[θaɪ]	Oberschenkel
space	[speɪs]	Weltall		thin	[θɪn]	dünn
spacecraft	[ˈspeɪsˌkrɑːft]	Raumschiff		thistle	[ˈθɪsl]	Distel
spade	[speɪd]	Spaten		thorn	[θɔːn]	Dorn
sparrow	[ˈspærəʊ]	Spatz		thread	[θred]	Faden
spider	[ˈspaɪdə(r)]	Spinne		three	[θriː]	drei
to spill	[spɪl]	verschütten		thumb	[θʌm]	Daumen
spoon	[spuːn]	Löffel		thunderstorm	[ˈθʌndəstɔːm]	Gewitter
sport	[spɔːt]	Sport		thursday	[ˈθɜːzdɪ]	Donnerstag
spring	[sprɪŋ]	Frühling		ticket	[ˈtɪkɪt]	Eintrittskarte
square	[skweə(r)]	Quadrat		tie	[taɪ]	Krawatte
to squash	[skwɒʃ]	quetschen		to tie	[taɪ]	schnüren
to squeeze	[skwiːz]	auspressen		tiger	[ˈtaɪɡə(r)]	Tiger
squirrel	[ˈskwɪrəl]	Eichhörnchen		tile	[taɪl]	Fliese
stable	[steɪbl]	Stall		time	[taɪm]	Zeit
stag	[stæɡ]	Hirsch		tiptoe	[ˈtɪptəʊ]	auf Zehenspitzen gehen
stallion	[ˈstælɪən]	Hengst		tired	[ˈtaɪəd]	müde
stamp	[stæmp]	Briefmarke		toad	[təʊd]	Kröte
to stand	[stænd]	stehen		toboggan	[təˈbɒɡən]	Rodel
star	[stɑː(r)]	Stern		toe	[təʊ]	Zehe
starfish	[ˈstɑːfɪʃ]	Seestern		toilet	[ˈtɔɪlɪt]	Toilette
to start	[stɑːt]	starten		tomato	[təˈmɑːtəʊ]	Tomate
steering wheel	[ˈstɪərɪŋˌwiːl]	Lenkrad		tongue	[tʌŋ]	Zunge
stem	[stem]	Stängel		tool	[tuːl]	Werkzeug
stone	[stəʊn]	Stein		tooth	[tuːθ]	Zahn
to stop	[stɒp]	stehen bleiben		toothbrush	[ˈtuːθbrʌʃ]	Zahnbürste
stopwatch	[ˈstɒpwɒtʃ]	Stoppuhr		toothpaste	[ˈtuːθpeɪst]	Zahnpasta
strawberry	[ˈstrɔːbrɪ]	Erdbeere		top	[tɒp]	Spitze
stream	[striːm]	Bach		tornado	[tɔːˈneɪdəʊ]	Wirbelsturm
string	[strɪŋ]	Schnur		toucan	[ˈtuːkæn]	Tukan
stripe	[straɪp]	Streifen		tourist	[ˈtəʊrɪst]	Tourist
submarine	[ˌsʌbməˈriːn]	U-Boot		towel	[ˈtaʊəl]	Handtuch
sugar	[ˈʃʊɡə(r)]	Zucker		town	[taʊn]	Stadt
summer	[ˈsʌmə(r)]	Sommer		toy	[tɔɪ]	Spielzeug
sun	[sʌn]	Sonne		tractor	[ˈtræktə(r)]	Traktor
sunday	[ˈsʌndɪ]	Sonntag		traffic	[ˈtræfɪk]	Verkehr
sunglasses	[ˈsʌnˌɡlɑːsɪz]	Sonnenbrille		train	[treɪn]	Zug
supermarket	[ˈsuːpəmɑːkɪt]	Supermarkt		transparent	[trænsˈpærənt]	durchsichtig
swan	[swɒn]	Schwan		trapeze	[trəˈpiːz]	Trapez
to swim	[swɪm]	schwimmen		tray	[treɪ]	Tablett
swimming pool	[ˈswɪmɪŋˌpuːl]	Schwimmbecken		treasure	[ˈtreʒə(r)]	Schatz
swing	[swɪŋ]	Schaukel		tree	[triː]	Baum
sword	[sɔːd]	Schwert		tree trunk	[ˈtriːˌtrʌŋk]	Baumstamm
synagogue	[ˈsɪnəɡɒɡ]	Synagoge		triangle	[ˈtraɪæŋɡl]	Dreieck
				trick	[trɪk]	Trick
T (Seite 78–84)				tricycle	[ˈtraɪsɪkl]	Dreirad
table	[ˈteɪbl]	Tisch		trophy	[ˈtrəʊfɪ]	Pokal
tadpole	[ˈtædpəʊl]	Kaulquappe		trousers	[ˈtraʊzəz]	Hose
tail	[teɪl]	Schwanz		truck	[trʌk]	Lastwagen
to take	[teɪk]	nehmen		trumpet	[ˈtrʌmpɪt]	Trompete
tall	[tɔːl]	groß		trunk	[trʌŋk]	Rüssel
tambourine	[ˌtæmbəˈriːn]	Tamburin		tuba	[ˈtjuːbə]	Tuba
taxi	[ˈtæksɪ]	Taxi		Tuesday	[ˈtjuːzdɪ]	Dienstag
tea	[tiː]	Tee		tugboat	[ˈtʌɡˌbəʊt]	Schlepper

103

A B C D E F G H I J K L M N O P Q R S T U V W X Y Z

tulip	[ˈtjuːlɪp]	Tulpe
tunnel	[ˈtʌnl]	Tunnel
turkey	[ˈtɜːkɪ]	Truthahn
turtle	[ˈtɜːtl]	Schildkröte
tusk	[tʌsk]	Stoßzahn
twig	[twɪg]	Zweig
twin	[twɪn]	Zwilling
two	[tuː]	zwei
typewriter	[ˈtaɪpˌraɪtə(r)]	Schreibmaschine

U (Seite 84)

umbrella	[ʌmˈbrelə]	Regenschirm
uncle	[ˈʌŋkl]	Onkel
under	[ˈʌndə(r)]	unter
underwear	[ˈʌndəweə(r)]	Unterwäsche
to undress	[ʌnˈdres]	umziehen
unicorn	[ˈjuːnɪkɔːn]	Einhorn
university	[juːnɪˈɜːsətɪ]	Universität
up	[ʌp]	hinauf
Uranus	[jʊˈreɪnəs]	Uranus

V (Seite 85–86)

vacuum cleaner	[ˈvækjʊəmˌkliːnə(r)]	Staubsauger
valley	[ˈvælɪ]	Tal
valve	[vælv]	Ventil
vase	[vaːz]	Vase
vegetable	[ˈvedʒɪtəbl]	Gemüse
vehicle	[ˈviːɪkl]	Fahrzeug
Venus	[ˈviːnəs]	Venus
vet	[vet]	Tierarzt
videotape	[ˈvɪdɪoʊˌteɪp]	Videocassette
videorecorder	[ˈvɪdɪoʊˌteɪprɪˈkɔːdə(r)]	Videorecorder
village	[ˈvɪlɪdʒ]	Dorf
vine	[vaɪn]	Wein
vineyard	[ˈvɪnjəd]	Weinberg
violet	[ˈvaɪələt]	violett
violin	[ˌvaɪəˈlɪn]	Violine
volcano	[vɒlˈkeɪnəʊ]	Vulkan
vulture	[ˈvʌltʃə(r)]	Geier

W (Seite 86–90)

wagon	[ˈwægən]	Karren
waist	[weɪst]	Taille
waiter	[ˈweɪtə(r)]	Bedienung
to walk	[wɔːk]	gehen
walking stick	[ˈwɔːkɪŋˌstɪk]	Spazierstock
wall	[wɔːl]	Wand
wallaby	[ˈwɒləbɪ]	Wallaby, kl. Känguru
wallet	[ˈwɒlɪt]	Geldbörse
walrus	[ˈwɔːlrəs]	Walross
to want	[wɒnt]	wollen
to wash	[wɒʃ]	waschen
watch	[wɒtʃ]	Uhr
to watch	[wɒtʃ]	betrachten
water	[ˈwɔːtə(r)]	Wasser
waterfall	[ˈwɔːtəfɔːl]	Wasserfall
waterlily	[ˈwɔːtəlɪlɪ]	Seerose
watermelon	[ˈwɔːtəmelən]	Wassermelone
to wave	[weɪv]	winken
to wear	[weə(r)]	tragen
wedding	[ˈwedɪŋ]	Hochzeit
Wednesday	[ˈwenzdɪ]	Mittwoch
week	[wiːk]	Woche
to weigh	[weɪ]	wiegen
to wet	[wet]	feucht
whale	[weɪl]	Wal
wheat	[wiːt]	Weizen
wheel	[wiːl]	Rad
wheelbarrow	[ˈwiːlˌbærəʊ]	Schubkarren
wheelchair	[ˈwiːlˌtʃeə(r)]	Rollstuhl

wish	[wɪʃ]	wünschen
whiskers	[ˈwɪskəz]	Schnurrhaare
to whisper	[ˈwɪspə(r)]	flüstern
whistle	[ˈwɪsl]	Pfeife
white	[waɪt]	weiß
wide	[waɪd]	breit
wife	[waɪf]	Ehefrau
will	[wɪl]	werden
wind	[wɪnd]	Wind
windmill	[ˈwɪndmɪl]	Windmühle
window	[ˈwɪndəʊ]	Fenster
wing	[wɪŋ]	Flügel
winter	[ˈwɪntə(r)]	Winter
wire	[ˈwaɪə(r)]	Draht
witch	[wɪtʃ]	Hexe
wizard	[ˈwɪzəd]	Zauberer
wolf	[wʊlf]	Wolf
woman	[ˈwʊmən]	Frau
women	[ˈwɪmɪn]	Frauen
wood	[wʊd]	Holz
wool	[wʊl]	Wolle
world	[wɜːld]	Welt
worm	[wɜːm]	Wurm
wrinkle	[ˈrɪŋkl]	Falte
wrist	[rɪst]	Handgelenk
write	[raɪt]	schreiben

X (Seite 90)

X-Ray	[ˈeksreɪ]	Röntgenaufnahme
xylophone	[ˈzaɪləfəʊn]	Xylofon

Y (Seite 91)

yacht	[jɒt]	Yacht
to yawn	[jɔːn]	gähnen
year	[jɜː(r)]	Jahr
yellow	[ˈjeləʊ]	gelb
yoghurt	[ˈjɒgət]	Joghurt
yolk	[jəʊk]	Eigelb
young	[jʌŋ]	jung

Z (Seite 91)

zebra	[ˈziːbrə]	Zebra
zero	[ˈzɪərəʊ]	null
zip	[zɪp]	Reißverschluss
zoo	[zuː]	Zoo

Danksagungen
Dorling Kindersley dankt folgenden Personen für die Unterstützung bei der Herstellung dieses Buches:
Lektorat Nicola Tuxworth, Bildgestaltung Rowena Alsey, Umschlaggestaltung Karen Lieberman, Bildrecherche Jenny Rayner und Sarah Moule, Design Mark Richards, Nicky Simmonds und Sharon Peters

Bildnachweis
o = oben, u = unten, l = links, r = rechts, m = Mitte
Aquila / A. Cooper 22or; Bruce Coleman Ltd / E. & P. Bauer 84ol, M. Freeman 19mu; L. Lee Rue 37 mlu; M. P. Kahl 16 ul; H. Reinhard 26mro; K. Tanaka (WWF) 55ur; FLPA / E. & D. Hosking 42ur, 87ul; NHPA /O. Rogge 24mlo; OSF / J. A. L. Cooke 50mlo; Science Photo Library / T. Craddock 68ur; Survival Anglia / M. Day 33ol

Fotos
Simon Battensby, Jon Boucher, Paul Bricknell, Jane Burton, Peter Chadwick, Gordon Clayton, Antony Cooper, Geoff Dann, Philip Dowell, Michael Dunning, Andreas Einsiedel, Jo Foord, Philip Gatward, Paul Goff, Frank Greenaway, Stephen Hayward, Colin Keates, Dave King, Bob Langrish, Cyril Laubscher, Ray Moller, David Murry, Stephen Oliver, Daniel Pangbourne, Roger Philips, Suzanna Price, Karl Shone, Steve Shott, Clive Streeter, Kim Taylor, Mathew Ward, Paul Williams, Jerry Young.

Zusätzliche Danksagungen
Sarah Ashun und Agry Ombler – Photoassistenz; Sue Wookey – Bildersuche; Blindenhunde für die Blinden; Great Ormond Street Hospital für die Krücken; Design Studio, Reigate für die Fliese, James Smith&Sons (Umbrellas) Ltd. für den Spazierstock; The Bead Shop, Covent Garden für den Schatz; Nigel Busch für das Motorrad, Rank Film Distributors Ltd. für den Film, Kentish Town City Farm für die Bereitstellung der Kuh und des Kalbes zum Photographieren; Frank Barnes School, Julians Primary School und Columbia Road Primary School dafür, dass sie Schülern erlaubt haben, in diesem Buch zu erscheinen; Schüler und Lehrer der Winnersh Primary School, The Coombes at Arborfield, und Columbia Road Primary School für den Feldversuch mit dem »Ersten Wörterbuch« während der Produktion.